SECRETS
FOR A
SUCCESSFUL
DISSERTATION

This book is dedicated
with heartfelt appreciation to
Barry
D.L.
and
Phyllis

SECRETS FOR A SUCCESSFUL DISSERTATION

Jacqueline Fitzpatrick
Jan Secrist
Debra J. Wright

SAGE Publications
International Educational and Professional Publisher
Thousand Oaks   London   New Delhi

For information:

 SAGE Publications, Inc.
2455 Teller Road
Thousand Oaks, California 91320
E-mail: order@sagepub.com

SAGE Publications Ltd.
6 Bonhill Street
London EC2A 4PU
United Kingdom

SAGE Publications India Pvt. Ltd.
M-32 Market
Greater Kailash I
New Delhi 110 048 India

Printed in the United States of America

Library of Congress Cataloging-in-Publication Data

Fitzpatrick, Jacqueline.
    Secrets for a successful dissertation / Jacqueline Fitzpatrick, Jan Secrist,
    Debra J. Wright.
        p.   cm.
    Includes index.
    ISBN 0-7619-1250-9 (cloth: acid-free paper)
    ISBN 0-7619-1251-7 (pbk.: acid-free paper)
        1. Dissertations, Academic. 2. Research—Methodology. I. Secrist,
    Jan. II. Wright, Debra J. III. Title.
    LB2369.S383 1998
        808′.02—dc21   98-8899

This book is printed on acid-free paper.

98 99 00 01 02 03 10 9 8 7 6 5 4 3 2

Acquiring Editor:	Harry Briggs
Editorial Assistant:	Anna Howland
Production Editor:	Sherrise M. Purdum
Typesetter/Designer:	Janelle LeMaster
Indexer:	Teri Greenberg
Print Buyer:	Anna Chin

Contents

Part II: The Secrets to Maintaining Sanity and Good Humor

Foreword

Secrets for a Successful Dissertation is one of the most thorough, incisive, and, above all, honest books on the perils of the doctoral student that I have had the pleasure of reading. The authors, who have spent many collective years perfecting this volume, show uncanny wisdom and abundant humor as they portray the often perilous route doctoral students must take to succeed in the graduate school role. Their portrait reveals many of the "unspoken" norms that doctoral students face. They have researched current and contemporary literature in methodology, psychology, and stress and time management. The net result is a book that is highly readable, thought-provoking, and, especially, entertaining. I found myself laughing and crying at the same time, thinking, "Thank god I survived the process." It covers just about everything a reader would wish to know about the trek to obtaining a doctoral degree. It covers specific graduate school hurdles, pitfalls, and what to do about them and retain your sanity at the same time. Their analysis is insightful and tinged with specific applications and examples that facilitate the process of not only surviving but thriving in a graduate school.

Johanna Steggert Hunsaker, Ph.D.
Professor of Organizational Behavior
University of San Diego

Acknowledgments

We thank the following for their consistent encouragement throughout this challenging process:

- Harry Briggs, our editor, for his enthusiasm, ready responsiveness, and clear understanding of our message

- The Sage staff and patient problem-solvers willing to work with three strong-willed women

- Johanna Hunsaker, Ph.D., who offered critical guidance and introduction to the publishing world

- Kathy Heinrich, Ph.D., whose passion for research and writing inspired us to complete this manuscript

- The faculty and students who are familiar with this process, shared a variety of stories, and have requested anonymity

- Our patient families, who keep asking, "Is it done yet?" and "What will you dream up to do next?"

Introduction

Great Expectations

It was the best of times, it was the worst of times.
—Charles Dickens

Are you contemplating going back to school for a doctorate? Or are you well beyond the contemplation stage, far enough through the course work to think you might actually finish and now facing the mysteries of the dissertation phase? Or perhaps you know brave folks who are currently leaping over endless academic hurdles and tearing out their hair from the isolation and lack of information stages that pass for the "dissertation phase." If you are personally seeking a Ph.D., an Ed.D., or Psy.D. or know anyone who is, you are reading the right book.

Writing a dissertation is guaranteed to reduce former academic confidence levels to quivering attacks of feeling "educationally challenged." Straight A's on your transcript do not guarantee your success in the dissertation process; those grades only tell you that you have mastered the art of chew, swallow, and regurgitate what each professor believes is important. Glowing comments on your weekly critique papers don't guarantee you will write a sentence that will pass muster with your dissertation committee. In other words, all your work up to this point does not seem to have a great deal of bearing on the writing of a dissertation.

Writing a dissertation is much like writing a book, and it is an exhilarating accomplishment. The benefits jump out immediately: a better advantage in the job market, being introduced in social situations and seeing the "wow" in people's expressions, improved chances of future publication, receiving greater consideration for your ideas, and finally being able to relax and enjoy life.

Secrets for a Successful Dissertation has been written by three women who have recently completed doctoral degrees in educational leadership. This information is offered to both women and men, obviously, but we simply cannot help a bit of gender bias—how can it be otherwise? Even though this book tends to lean toward the soft sciences, certain chapters will also aid those struggling in the more traditional, that is, hard, sciences. Debra Sikes (1996) reported that women earned more doctorates than men in education and, for the first time, in social sciences, but men surpassed women in every other field. We also have read that many women enter various doctoral programs with higher college GPAs but lower candidacy and graduation rates. We would like to boost those graduation rates for women. However, because we also like men, we would like to boost their graduation rates as well. We recognize that the work requirements for dissertations are (or should be) the same and yet the results, regardless of gender, are wildly different. This is neither a gender nor an age issue, it is a student issue. Thus we have included advice from students and graduates of both genders, all ages, varied ethnic groups, and many disciplines from universities in diverse parts of the country. We recommend you read this book in its entirety, then revisit each chapter when you get down in the dumps and have nothing better to do.

We often felt there must be secret passageways through the doctoral program that we had to stumble onto ourselves, like a torturous adolescent rite of passage with all the insecurities but none of the acne. Academia can be as silent and as difficult to move as an elephant in your living room. So we offer this book in an effort at least to get that elephant's attention so you can point it in the right direction. The rest is up to you.

The chapter and section titles have been joyfully borrowed and tweaked from every famous book or movie we can think of, for no redeeming reason other than to make you smile. You need to smile. Believe us, you need smiles. We also added commonly found road signs to remind you that these are well-traveled roads.

Who are we? We are the coauthors, but because we felt more like conspirators for much of the writing process, we refer to ourselves as co-conspirators. Neither our stories nor our lives are limited to titles, so we provide the following, in our own words.

Dr. Jacqueline Fitzpatrick: I expected the writing of the dissertation to be the highlight of my graduate experience. My dissertation subject, an examination of the mentoring relationship between two women, continues to be an important topic to me. Even though my interest in my topic never wavered, I found the dissertation process filled with invigorating highs and frustrating lows. I discovered I shared similar experiences with other doctoral students. Looking back, I can say that many of my disappointments could and should have been avoided. As savvy as I considered myself to be, I lacked some simple knowledge that I now have. Some experiences were uplifting: uncovering fascinating data from research participants, trying to maintain the library rules of silence when I discovered a vital snippet of information, reviewing the completion of each chapter, accepting an encouraging word from a committee member, and hearing positive feedback that the research truly made a difference in women's lives. My purpose for writing this book is to help you focus on your topic, understand the dissertation process, remind you to keep your sense of humor, and not let yourself become overwhelmed by lack of knowledge of political and personality issues that should have no bearing on your timely graduation.

Co-conspirator opinion: "Jacque is the organizational glue that holds our support group together on assigned tasks. She is the master of typed class notes, the superorganizer of manuscripts, and is highly (and ever so tactfully) skilled in 'the taming of the shrews.' "

Dr. Jan Secrist: My midlife journey through a doctoral program was mostly for curiosity and to satisfy a personal challenge, which I am delighted to say I accomplished. The journey also created two opposing insights. First, I rediscovered that my personality prefers to revel in wonder of words, not wrestle with rigid thinking patterns, and that I'd much rather explore the inner personalities of people than the outer trappings of power. Second, the journey squelched most of my natural voice for three years. At the beginning of the program I was told, "Don't put a smile in your writing." When I responded that I'd spent many years being paid to put a smile in my writing, the answer was, "Not acceptable in a doctoral program." Slowly, semester after semester, the regimented classes chipped off chunks of my personal voice, dulling its sparkle and denting my time-honored, off-beat sense of humor. Fortunately, a couple of classes encouraged an occasional rebellious squeak of independence. Near the end of the program I was relieved to discover that my irreverent, maverick voice was returning, which allowed me to thoroughly enjoy writing the dissertation. I cowrote this book in hopes that its upbeat message will encourage others to play the academic game honestly—but always hold firm to their individuality, speak their own language, and honor their own voices.

Co-conspirator opinion: "We keep Jan around because she's our persistent humorist and satirist. She forces us to enjoy life and its failings. She is the master of the questions 'Why?' and 'Why not?' and keeps the party going."

Dr. Debra J. Wright: As the person who planned to graduate the day after Orientation, I found myself struggling through this dissertation process as a novice, fighting for sanity, wondering why I ever began, and yet always knowing there was a light (although at times very dim) at the end of the tunnel. Completion of the doctoral dissertation, and ultimately the degree, was as much of a necessity, careerwise, as it was a stepping stone to competence, self-esteem, and the very real feeling that life begins after 40! So many around me had yet to begin the process and so many who went before me had yet to end the process. There was a passion as well as a sense of achievement in meeting this goal and looking in the mirror each morning and realizing I had no more apologies to make for my intelligence and no more extraneous initials to intimidate me in the hallowed halls of academia. My purpose for this book was to open the door to humor as well as to reinforce to others that this is not a matter of intelligence. This process is a matter of persistence, diligence, and tolerance for ancient rituals that make one stand out in a crowd (not to be confused with outstanding in your own field) and more personally a reward to myself and my family in finally accepting what they kept telling me all along: You can do it. I didn't quite graduate the day after Orientation, but I did break some records.

Co-conspirator opinion: "Debbie is so incredibly smart, she makes the rest of us look terrific, so of course we hang out with her. Her sense of humor, fast repartee, and amazing depth of knowledge add much needed balance to head off our perpetual 'comedy of errors.' "

The three of us have found certain truths to be self-evident in our academic journeys. Whether you are researching people or plants, microbiology or moon shots, prejudices or preferences, irregular cell division or erratic fatty substitutes, intelligence quotients or emotional quirks, or anything else under the umbrella of what passes for research these days, you will find that there are rules—strict rules, often listed as "guidelines." You may love them or think they are archaic, pedantic, endless, and unreasonable rules. But you must follow them to the letter. Because different universities have slightly different rules, it is up to you to fine-tune your information gathering to your own university. It is also true, however, that dissertations have many common elements no matter where you are flexing your doctoral "wanna-be" ambitions. These general concepts are what we address in this book.

We can't solve all your academic and personal problems, negotiate your rule-solving, pay your bills, or write your dissertation. But we hope this tome offers some salient hints for surviving the dissertation process with your mind and body relatively intact. The average "recovery" time for most students completing a doctoral program is one to three years. Perhaps this book will not only shorten your recovery time but give you a sense of being in control of your own destiny along the way.

A novel and far-fetched idea, we know—but worth a try.

Reference

Sikes, D. (1996, May). In her own words: Warning: Getting a Ph.D. is hazardous to your health. *Women in Higher Education,* p. 17.

Part I

The Secrets of the Dissertation Content and Process

1

Writing the Doctoral Proposal

(aka The Birth of a Nation)

The road narrows as you begin the doctoral dissertation and develop your proposal. This is when you begin to understand the wise person who claimed, "Life shrinks or expands in proportion to one's courage." It does indeed take courage to launch yourself into this time-honored task of searching for the supposed approval of your topic and methodology of your research. The proposal often becomes the focal point for your self-esteem, the impetus to continue this journey, and an overall affirmation of your self-worth and value as a doctoral candidate. It can be a joyful occasion, and most proposals are. It is only as you work through what you thought was approved that you find out that some committee members are forgetful, or seemingly uncaring, and often change their minds as unpredictably as the winds blow their way through the changing seasons.

Obviously, you should carefully review the selection of committee members. This crucial step not only will be your salvation but can also easily turn into your worst nightmare. The strategies you employ in selecting your committee need to reflect your own personal strengths and weaknesses as well as your writing style. But before you begin to seriously select your committee members and chair, you will need to have a good concept of what you are undertaking.

Getting to the Topic and Its Focus (aka The Prelude)

You may have spent a number of years answering questions about the research that you will be doing for your dissertation. You may even have started saving some articles and notes in a broad and general sense. Now you need to focus and define your topic. There's no easy way to figure out your direct and absolute focus but there are some strategies that may work for you in refining your research. If you are having trouble stating in a few sentences what you are doing your dissertation on, then you will have to tighten your subject matter. Try writing an introduction to your first chapter. Looking at the broader picture often helps you reframe your special emphasis.

If that task is a bit terrifying at this point, try writing your research questions or objectives. By identifying and putting this material into actual written form, you can sometimes begin to see the direction and specificity of what you want to examine. In quantitative proposals, writing the null hypotheses is usually a fairly simple task because they are very concrete and address the issue in smaller pieces. If you are working on a qualitative proposal, there are some common words and phrases used in research questions. Terms such as *lived experiences, patterns, themes,* and *common characteristics* are a few that should spark your creative juices.

If you still are unsure of what eventual direction your research will take, then write up a one-page outline that you can present to potential committee members. This gives you and them a starting point for discussion. Decide beforehand why you are asking these specific people to serve on your committee. It is wise to supplement your areas of weakness with someone who can constructively help you. Finally, share with them your thoughts about your topic, why you are interested in that area, why it is important to you and your field or discipline. You may find that in these discussions, you are better able to put your thinking into writing. Be prepared for multiple drafts of everything. No one gets it right the first time through and now that you have involved three or more people who often won't agree, you will need to adapt a strong and somewhat detached perspective.

When choosing your topic, remember that it must be something that you are passionate about and that will maintain your interest for a long period of time. One of our professors said it better than we can.

YOUR HEROIC JOURNEY

There are two schools of conventional wisdom about dissertation topics. The first school advises that the best dissertation is a done dissertation, so do something quick and dirty. The second recommends that you love your dissertation topic because you will be living with it for a long time. A worthwhile dissertation has a passionate scholar behind it. To determine whether or not you are a passionate scholar, answer these three questions. Are you powerfully attracted to a particular topic because of a personal experience? Do you feel vulnerable speaking about this topic because of your intense personal investment in the topic? Are you grappling with how to transform your passionate topic into an "acceptable" dissertation format that a committee could sanction?

If you answered yes to one or more of these questions, you probably are a passionate scholar. Passionate dissertation scholarship is personally and socially meaningful research that explores a phenomenon or the experiences of a group of people about whom one cares deeply. Conducting passionate scholarship is a heroic journey that challenges the doctoral scholar personally and academically.

If you are drawn to a passionate topic, recognize that yours will be a heroic journey populated by both allies and dragons. You will need allies to create a community of scholarly caring for yourself in your doctoral program. This community can be made up of student colleagues and faculty members who mentor and support your ideas. By creating a network of allies, passionate scholars will be better prepared to meet the dragons who inevitably appear along the way in the journey toward graduation.

From K. T. Heinrich, Ph.D.,
Associate Professor, University of Hartford
Reprinted with permission.

A few strategic questions can guide your thinking: What have you always wondered about? Is there something you discovered during one of your classes that you always promised yourself you would look into further? What area of expertise would you like to be known for at the conclusion of your program? What could/ would you speak about to other groups with similar interests, present at a conference, or write/publish an article about?

As soon as you are set on a topic or area of interest, you will need to formulate ideas about your methodology. And, yes, we all have to have a methodology of choice. Don't take on a methodological strategy that doesn't fit your style, and don't take on a methodology that doesn't fit your topic. Also, be cognizant of preferences or prejudices your university or department has regarding different methodologies. It can be very upsetting to have a committee whose only background is in statistical treatments and analysis trying to understand you and your qualitative research on the lifestyles of the rich and famous.

A good strategy at this point is to read and review your institution's doctoral handbook to see if there are guidelines about what goes into the proposal, when and if you have to provide copies before your defense date, and how long it is expected to be. Our institution decided proposals should be no longer than 30 pages, and that's for the first three chapters. Typically, Chapter One is titled the "Problem" (or Statement of the Problem), Chapter Two, "Review of Literature," and Chapter Three, "Methodology." You can hardly begin to review the literature in that amount of space but institutions like their own rules. A chair is the ultimate thumbs-up or thumbs-down person. Talk with him or her at great length, take him or her to lunch, meet for coffee, get him or her out of the office and enjoy some relational time while you ask those pesky, bothersome questions that plague many of us at the beginning.

Writing the Proposal (aka Pygmalion)

It is just plain ridiculous if you are going to do this much work not to do the best job you can in preparing your proposal. The best of all worlds is that after you conduct your research, your Chapters One, Two, and Three will only need minor revisions to be ready for the final dissertation. Even if you have to edit and cut portions due to page limitations, you can and should be writing the proposal and the dissertation at the same time. You will find nothing more discouraging than having to spend more time on the Internet, make more journeys to the university library, and burn up more hours struggling with rewriting or adding to what you have already done. Warning to qualitative researchers: You may have to do this anyway as your data emerges.

The development of each individual chapter has specific components and deals with somewhat separate issues, but keep in mind that when your chapters come together they must present a whole, leading into each other in some kind of an organized writing schemata. You may want to review and keep handy the appendix to this book that has a checklist for the items and headings typically found in a dissertation (see the Emergency Appendectomies section). There have been students who look upon each chapter as an individual paper or essay, and when it is time to pull it all together, they find they have a great murder mystery with no ending, no clue as to who the culprit is, and no pattern or theme for even the most ardent detective to follow. So take care in always thinking long range and long term. The best advice overheard by a fellow doctoral student working on his dissertation was that each chapter had three distinct sections: the Introduction, where you tell them what you are going to tell them; the Body, where you actually tell them; and the Summary, where you then tell them what you already told them.

Some aspects of dissertations are rote and quite academic. If you have done your homework and looked through completed dissertations, you will see the academic language that is used in beginning each chapter with an introduction and in ending each chapter with a summary or conclusion. It doesn't take reinventing the English language to follow this type of format. It is not plagiarism because it is expected that there will be similarities in the form and format of writing. Your life and your writing will not be your own, literally, until you have earned the right—as has been often said— in Chapter Five or Chapter Six of your dissertation. In most cases, Chapter Five is your "Summary, Conclusions, and Recommendations," although if you have unusual or extra material that begs to be placed in a separate chapter, your summary will become Chapter Six.

Keep your writing as interesting as possible. Throw in good quotations from recognized people in the field throughout Chapter One to keep your reader interested and prove that you know what you are talking about. This style of writing is not about creativity or casual writing, it is basically a defense and exercise in your ability to meet academic rigor established more than 100 years ago. Remember, you will have to defend every subjective statement you make. Your opinions at this point are worthless: You are just a struggling doctoral student, so what do you know? Find out if all your writing has to be in the third person form. Some institutions have a more qualitative leaning, letting the writer gain voice by actually using first person pronouns. Finally, remember that the proposal is all in the future tense because, technically, you have not been given permission even to begin this research effort. You are only humbly proposing your concepts and awaiting the divine blessing of your committee members at your proposal defense.

By the way, in case you have been breathlessly awaiting those ever helpful hints about the actual writing of the dissertation proposal, the rules, the styles, and even some samples, you can start breathing again. We have specifically chosen to ignore a tedious lecture on periods, commas, semicolons, dynamic opening sentences, and good writing habits. If you have made it this far in the academic world, it is safe to assume that you possess these skills in abundance. One word of warning here is that you should never expect someone's dissertation to be a template to success for you. There are many errors, many format faux pas, and many different styles in theses and dissertations. This is to be expected because there are many style manuals, and many universities, many departments and divisions, that each like to put their stamp on what they believe is the best method for reporting research. Is it a hierarchy? Yes, of course it is and you will be well aware by this time of the writing style and rules that are acceptable to your local institution.

It would also be disastrous to suggest to you that a single style of writing is better or preferred over any other style. The important criteria here are that the rules of English apply to all that you write, the rules and preferences of committee members apply to all that you write, and the rules of academic redundance apply in abundance to all that you write. If you have any doubts here, take a stroll through your local academic library and pull out any thesis or dissertation. You will see the same basic format, the same basic tenets of writing, and the same basic sameness throughout all these productions. If you still have questions, wander through your local bookstore and gaze upon all the books that offer so much specific advice and checklists and rules that you will be mind-boggled and wonder why you ever launched this project in the first place.

Perhaps this recipe of key ingredients will satisfy your cravings for academic fame and fortune:

RECIPE FOR DESSERT-ATION

Take one jar of cranial jam, seasoned three to seven years in ivory towers.

Pour into a mixing bowl (not to be confused with a toilet bowl) and add generous amounts of sweat and tears.

Fold in one pair of bifocals, a dozen student loan applications, and stir vigorously until rigor mortis sets in.

With a beater, blend in one pound of finely crushed perseverence along with one large IQ. (If you are out of the latter, a ton of tenacity will do.)

Add a pinch of gray hair (a bald spot will work as a substitute) and sprinkle in a handful of polysyllabic words. This will impress your friends and neighbors every time.

Place in an APA-style pan.

Marinate in pickle juice or other preservative and let it rise for six months. Punch down and let rise for another six months. If you cannot punch it down, don't worry, a dessert-ation committee will do it for you.

Finally, place the substance in a blue-cloth-bound cover and celebrate; you are the proud owner of a dessert-ation.

The result is a 1- to 2-inch-shelf-sufficient dust collector, enough to bore six to eight people at one seating, also usable as a miniature breadboard. This can be redeemed at local universities for a doctoral diploma, suitable for hanging and résumé padding (periodic dusting required). If this recipe does not turn out for you, don't worry, ABD (All But Dissertation) isn't the end of the world.

From Alan Nelson, Ed.D.,
Director of the Southwest Center
for Leadership, Scottsdale, AZ.
Reprinted with permission.

Reviewing the Literature (aka Awakening the Dead)

Now is when Literature Review Anxiety Syndrome kicks in, causing occasional twitching and jerking muscles. The best remedy is simply to work smart. You don't have to read every book that was ever published on your subject nor do you have to review every article in every journal or periodical. You may even want to start work on this chapter prior to your Chapter One as you will need to know what the field has been and is saying about your topic.

You will also need to know the "movers and shakers" in this particular area. You can't complete a literature review about the effectiveness of polio vaccines and not include a substantial discussion about the research of Jonas Salk. This will take time and more time and still more time until you are so thoroughly saturated and overloaded that you develop the Literature Review Anxiety Syndrome. This is where you are just so sure that you don't have everything you need, that you have missed something substantial, and that if you just allocate one more week in the library you will find that final missing piece. This syndrome is tantamount to wanting to locate the missing link or winning the lottery. It just ain't going to happen, so get over it. A good literature review comes from the patient accumulation of bits and pieces of research, and an obsessive-compulsive quality is indeed a valuable trait.

Talking about spending time in the library, you will quickly become familiar with all library bookshelves within your discipline and you will most likely be on a first-name basis with the librarians during this period of time. First you need to check out if there are any special library services afforded to doctoral students. Our institution initiated a policy that gave doctoral students 20 free articles and also, through the intervention of one of our classmates and a friendly letter, we were allowed to keep library books for six months. We also were given the opportunity to sit down with a library research associate who was willing to help us locate references (more on this story in Chapter 7, the organization chapter). Take advantage of every free, time-saving service you can find.

Also, don't forget to share your dissertation topic with friends and fellow students; they will remember you when they see something and, more times than not, copy something for you that may turn out to be one of your vital missing links.

Time in the library can be well spent if you are active on the computer. You can call for references at home and even determine if the books are currently available. Sometimes doctoral students can also order interlibrary loan materials through their computers. But you will probably not get out of visits to the actual library facility. First and foremost, take the time for one of those pesky library orientations. If you find only one thing helpful to your research, it will be well worth your efforts. Libraries are quickly moving into the technology age and may have resources you did not know about the last time you dragged yourself through their hallowed halls. Also, be sure to check out any computer access limits. Some institutions schedule time on the computer databases and you can call ahead to schedule individual access.

Be prepared to spend time sitting on the floor and looking at every book on a shelf. It's almost impossible to find a book on leadership when the author has chosen to title the book *Teaching the Elephants to Dance,* but if you find the leadership shelf, you will find multiple resources on the same shelf (thank goodness for the Dewey Decimal System). Carefully choose only those books you actually want to spend more time with at home; leave the others for the poor, unfortunate other doctoral student who has not read this book.

In reviewing books, first scan the table of contents and identify if the whole book or just portions of it may be useful to you. If you get no clues from that section, turn to the index for your key words. If you are only interested in a certain portion of a book, skim through the foreword. Most authors are adept at putting in the themes of each chapter and section, and you can narrow down what you want more quickly and also save yourself from having to haul around a shopping bag full of books. If you have ultimately decided to check out an entire book, then take the time at home to investigate each chapter. Start with the introduction to the chapter; it often outlines the key points to be made. Then go to the end of that chapter and read the summary. You can then decide if it is worth your valuable time to read through the whole chapter.

An additional note at this point is that you should always carry large amounts of change when traveling to the library. You will become close friends with the copy machine, and it eats coins faster than you can yank them out of your pockets. Most libraries have change machines, but don't count on them. Does your university library have any great deals on copy cards? Often if you are going to copy substantial amounts of paper over a period of time, it is cheaper per copy to prepurchase copies by buying a card. It can sometimes save you up to two cents per copy. And don't forget periodicals; their cost will make a serious dent in your weekly food budget.

In searching for periodicals, you first need to identify those journals that your department or school finds to be noteworthy for your discipline. This is a better place to start than just doing a random ERIC search. Most journals and periodicals will devote a single issue to a specific topic. You can find a wealth of information if you are fortunate enough to identify this issue. Also take the time to review the annual indexes of journals, which outline the author and name of the article for the entire year. You'll hit a bonanza if you can find a synopsis or synthesis of the literature on the topic you are investigating. You'll probably develop the Squinty Microfilm Eye Syndrome at this time, but eventually your eyesight will return to normal.

Another very handy resource is the bibliography or reference section of any article or book. Take the time to copy it when you are interested in a particular book or article, as it can serve a two-fold purpose. One, you now have the actual cited reference to use should you lose your original notes or not copy the salient information, and, two, you also have another great resource for further references. If someone else has gone to the trouble of locating all these references, you might as well benefit from their use.

This leads to two final, relatively unknown and unused sources for your review of the literature: the doctoral dissertation and the reference materials section in your library. Think for a moment about what you are trying to accomplish: an exhaustive review of the literature for your dissertation. Well, you may not have been the only one ever to do this. Look in your library's listing of doctoral dissertations: If a title even remotely sounds of the same nature as yours, get it and go right to its reference section. Someone has already begun the journey that you are now embarking on; that's one of the reasons that references are used, so others can verify and share in the bounty.

The second source is usually located in the reference materials section of your library. There are encyclopedias for most disciplines that list almost every topic you can think of. The great thing about these is that someone has gone to the trouble to provide a somewhat historical perspective on a multitude of topics. That means they have sat for hours on the library floor researching the topics. You can gain valuable insights into the leaders in the field as well as get some idea of how their research was done and what critiques were made. You can't check these books out, but they are well worth the price of a cup of good coffee to copy and review later. Don't forget their references as a great source for follow-up of the original documents or readings.

Completion of the literature review is a big step in gaining you begrudging acceptance as a scholar by your committee. In fact, when you are finished, you will have read more current and up-to-date literature than they have and they know it.

Developing Your Methodology
(aka The Devil's Racetrack)

Chapter Three is your recipe, your plan, your step-by-step procedure in the process of undertaking your research. It is also the chapter that will include some appendix materials (i.e., survey instrument, consent form, interview guide, interview protocol). Because this chapter is much like Chapter One in that it is fairly concrete in the sections that need to be addressed, you would be wise to revisit other dissertations and carefully read this particular chapter. It may even be smart to review a dissertation in which your chair was a chair. This chapter often gets the most attention and the most (vocal) suggestions.

This may be another time to stop and examine the section in the appendix that gives more specifics to the writing of these sections (see the Emergency Appendectomies). In any case, this is where your defense may become a real defense. You will have to show that you have developed a sane and rational framework from which you are going to operate, including the protection of human subjects, the kind of population you are going to sample, the manner and means in which you will analyze your data, and why your choice of methodology may be limited. This chapter will also be the one that needs the most revision before you go to your final Chapter Three. It will need extensive tense changes and also may need revisions in your actual processes and procedures.

For those completing quantitative research, the writing of Chapter Three is almost rote. There is specific language to be used regarding levels of significance, the restatement of the hypotheses, data analysis, and limitations of the chosen statistical treatment. Again, checking out those who have gone before you will give you a jump start on this academic jargon. Qualitative proposals are often harder to fit into this chapter as there are many ambiguities and uncertainties about the actual data as they evolve. The best advice here, again, is to review completed dissertations. The abstract for the dissertation is a good place to determine the methodological approach that was used. In completing Chapter Three, you may be required to add an additional section that outlines your time line for completion of your research. Committees of all types like to see that you are not rushing into something, that you have planned enough time to address the "Pay Your Dues" Syndrome that many faculty in institutions of higher learning seem to be obsessed with. This section is a simple listing of your major tasks and anticipated completion dates for those tasks.

In completing the proposal, you will need to include your references or bibliography and any appendixes you have referred to. Now you are ready for the big date. This is as close to a dry run as you will get for observing the interaction of your committee members. It is important to pay particular attention to comments made during this defense. It is strongly advised that you (or someone you trust) tape-record the session for your own sanity and protection down the road—with committee permission, of course. You will be greatly relieved when this step is over. You should come out of your proposal defense bursting with enthusiasm and the confidence that finally, after all these years, your ideas and work have made the grade. You have been validated. Some doctoral students believe that the proposal defense is a more important milestone than the actual dissertation defense.

Proposal defenses usually don't last more than two excruciating hours. One of us nervously walked into the defense room, organized her papers and presentation, awaited the committee members, went through the formalities, and when the first word was uttered, the electricity in the building went out. Needless to say, in an enclosed trailer with windows that did not open, no air-conditioning, and no overhead projector, the defense lasted only 45 minutes. So, time is relative. The time for the proposal defense is more an issue of your preference. Are you better and more alert in the morning hours? Or are you one of those "I get more energy as the day progresses" people? The other important issue is when your committee can be available. Many proposal candidates strategically suggest a time in the early morning to avoid all those other curious doctoral candidates appearing at the defense. It is a time of nervous anxiety and you need to analyze whether you are better in crowds or almost alone, as your support group will certainly be present on the appointed day, even if you schedule February 29th as your date!

The completion of the defense proposal surely is a time for celebration and a rededication to the many months of work yet to come. Don't reinvent the wheel in terms of your proposal; work smart. Do as much literature review as you think is needed for your dissertation, whether it's contained within the proposal or not. You are now on your own, working on your dissertation, and if you've done your homework well, three-fifths of this process is under control.

SECRETS CHECKLIST

1. _____ Choose a topic that you can be passionate about.

2. _____ Now is the time to open your doctoral handbook and check protocol.

3. _____ Your choice of methodology influences writing style and form.

4. _____ Don't shortchange your proposal; write it as your opening chapters of the dissertation.

2

Choosing a Methodology

(aka A Tale of Two Methodologies)

Quant. or qual., qual. or quant.? Which way to go? It's like the proverbial fork in the road, and the direction you choose to take is crucial to your ultimate sanity level as well as your ability to sustain the hours and hours and hours you will spend with your data. In your choice of methodological strategy, data analysis is often the most exciting, most frustrating, most often revisited, most confusing, most lamented, most rewarding, most abundant "I'll never get it done" portion of your dissertation. Keep two major points in mind: (a) Be true to your view of the world and your life beliefs, and (b) make absolutely, positively sure that you thoroughly understand, can work with, over and over and over again without throwing your hands up in despair, your choice of methods to best accomplish your desired end result. When in doubt, try the method we co-conspirators used as we resorted to youthful problem-solving styles and broke into a frustrated chant of "Eeeny, meeny, miney, mo—Catch a method by the toe. If it hollers, let it go, eeeny, meeny, miney, mo."

Deciding Which Is Best
(aka The Hunt for Real October)

It would seem quite simple to make this choice but you will find that with all decisions, the road travels in two directions. What's in a name? The actual difference between the spelling of *qualitative* and *quantitative* is only two letters ("li" or "nt") but this difference is worlds apart in meaning, application, end results, purpose, structure, and your ability to do some critical self-diagnosis. If you are a person whose proclivities lean more toward anal retentiveness, concrete sequentiality, objectivity, number crunching, facts (not rumors), stability, logical positivism (seeking the facts or causes with little regard for subjective states), control and order, endless lists, and step-by-step processes and procedures, then you will probably need to remain true to your nature and use a quantitative methodological strategy.

If, on the other hand, you are a person who had great trouble in "stats" class, or thought the normal curve was a bend in the road, then you may find your true persuasion leans more toward qualitative research methodologies. If you find yourself always asking, "Why?" or saying to others, "But, what if?" if you are one of those persons who have trouble with true-false questions, if you can deal with a hundredfold times more data (real, rich, and deep, of course), if you are one of those people who talk, talk, talk, and can listen, listen, and listen, if you "cringe" at the thought of number crunching, and you really want to know what the "insider" view of things is, then you probably will need to choose a methodological strategy within the qualitative family.

Bear in mind, this family has some strange relatives and distant cousins whose intermarriages may have caused strange inbreeding that is questionable. This family tree includes some thick branches such as ethnography and phenomenology (if you can pronounce these on the first attempt, you probably have a winner), naturalistic inquiry and case study, grounded theory and hermeneutics (not to be confused with the hermeneutic dialectic circles family), and life histories, diary inquiries, narratives, and oral histories. This is only a beginning list of what the world of qualitative research has to offer those who venture into its realm. Then there are always the "black twigs" of the family tree that are not often mentioned, such as the historical studies branch.

Thus the Hunt for Real October begins as you decide which methodology fits who you are and what you are attempting to research. The goal should be a matter of fit between the situation under study and the best way to obtain conclusions from that study. There are strong prejudices in the various disciplines and fields for what is viewed as serious research, and you need to be highly cognizant of any leanings your university, college, or school as well as your chair and committee members may have in this regard.

To mix differences of opinion on methodological strategy is, frankly, to attempt suicide and not be successful. It's like trying to force the round peg into the square hole. It may even be like pitting your right brain against your left brain in a duel at high noon that can't be won by either side. This can be a lose-lose situation if you haven't done your homework and made some critical analysis of who you are, how you operate, and what you believe. To add to this turmoil are the three or more persons who will control your life over the duration of this process (your committee, of course) and may provide little direction or too much direction that only derails your journey. You'll discover you are the caboose at the wrong end of the train when faced with your ultimate challenge, the Big D.

What Do You Want to Research?
(aka The Heart of the Matter)

Choosing your methodological strategy is highly dependent upon your choice of topic and your research questions/objectives as well as your hypotheses. Small, specific research questions answer larger issues. As a student you will find it far easier to work with "bite-size" projects that can be completed in your lifetime. If you are trying to focus on perceptions and experiences of people and what they say they believe, the feelings they express, and the explanations they give, then you are finding significant realities (and, yes, that is multiple realities). When your data emerges as a result of your study or your first job is to find out what your second job is, then your research will involve qualitative methods.

Candidates for doctoral degrees at this point often ask, "Well, if this is true, how can I then write and defend a proposal when everything is supposed to emerge?" This is a good question and the ultimate answer lies in using the language of your method. You will end up with lots of holistic descriptions in your Chapter Three about your methodology. You will use such words as *themes, patterns,* and *commonalities.* Your research may be ungeneralizable and lack validity as well as reliability and thus it should. These last two terms are often associated with quantitative studies and one must be very careful not to let anyone try to quantify your qualitative research.

There is a subtle way to derail this tactic that surfaces when your committee asks for charts and graphs, when they ask how many, when they ask for more particulars, and when you propose a single case study and someone asks, "Why can't you interview 10 to 15 more people?" This is when you desperately try to meet these needs but they are not true to your original frame of reference or your choice of methodology.

Qualitative research assumes multiple constructions of reality, or no one single truth. It is a systematic, empirical strategy (although there are many in the "hard" sciences who would argue with you on this point) for answering questions about people in a bounded social context. Qualitative is a means for describing and attempting to understand observed regularities, patterns, commonalities, and/or themes in what people do, say, and report as their experience.

There are differences in the application of the scientific process in terms of how you will define your sample, develop your hypotheses, gather your data, analyze your collected data, and present your results. There are opportunities to cross-validate your data through methods of triangulation (most of these include using some quantitative strategies and they often will soothe the frustrated committee member who is strong on quantitative measures and skeptical about the whole qualitative process). Important components of most qualitative strategies are bias, interview protocol, interview guides, observation strategies, and consent forms. This chapter is not meant to advise you on all of these, only to alert you to the many areas you will need to address and be accountable for in terms of qualitative strategies.

Another "strange attractor" (to borrow from Margaret Wheatley) of the choice of a qualitative methodology is that of researcher bias. If you have already decided what your outcomes will be, if you can already state your conclusions and recommendations, or if your working title includes something like "The Positive Effects of . . . ," then you are suffering from researcher bias. You cannot go into a qualitative research design with preconceived notions. This is very hard, as we all have some "gut-level" instincts that bubble to the surface when we begin interviewing or working with the research of our passion. You must realize that your interview questions are more of a "Tell me about . . ." "Can you give me an example of . . ." "Would you clarify or expand on that . . ." issue than one of "Do you agree that . . ." "I've always thought . . ." or "A checklist of questions that must be answered." The best advice is to practice interviewing and really listen to what your participants are saying. There are many books available that can assist you in developing the right mind-set for qualitative research. The findings in your research should surprise you at least in one area. You are the instrument in this research symphony, not the whole woodwind section. First chair is assigned to your participant.

On the other hand, if your topic is to look at the measurable effects of a treatment or to look at attributes, differences, or change over a period of time given some baseline data, then you have defined more of a quantitative methodology. Many issues and topics can go either way, given your use of the language and how you actually structure your data collection and how you choose to analyze your data. You may want to think in terms of outcome orientations versus process orientations: whether you are assuming a dynamic or stable reality, and whether you as the researcher are removed from the data, with an outsider perspective, or close to the data, with an insider perspective.

Quantitative strategies also have many relatives and strange twisting branches to contend with. The family tree for this domain includes important limbs of relationship versus difference, with cousins of chi-square, t-test, regression, analysis of variance, correlation, and, of course, dichotomous, categorical variables (not to be confused with independent and dependent variables). There are post hoc findings to deal with, secondary hypotheses, interaction variables, levels of significance, and the granddaddy of all: How do you put the actual tables into your text in the proper form and format?

Much like its distant relative, quantitative strategies have to be defined in terms of specific outcomes. Not only do you need to understand the fine points between differences and relationships, you will need a talking vocabulary about threats to internal and external validity, robustness of your statistical treatment, Type 1 and Type 2 errors, points of central tendency, standard error of the means, dispersion and deviation, as well as the width of the spread. Then you have the added complication of determining whether you are using parametric or nonparametric techniques, whether you have a true experimental design, a quasi-experimental design, or an ex post facto design. Knowing the language for quantitative studies is an absolute necessity.

In terms of analyzing your data and presenting your findings, you are in better shape with quantitative studies because the data do not lie, unless, of course, you have input your data incorrectly and then you will be in significance hell. There have been cases of students who design outstanding surveys or research procedures or treatments, but they forget to collect data in terms of demographic, categorical variables. What follows are some great results but nothing to define or compare the data with in terms of a statistical treatment. A clue to this is when you ask the computer program to analyze your findings via a *t*-test or ANOVA and the window pops back up on the screen, "You need a *y* variable"; then, after a loud wail of frustration, you will know of which we speak.

Many doctoral students choose to hire stats experts to build their databases and input their data. This often includes a running of the data. Often an "expert" data analysis will appease those committee members who might be wary of your stats skills and competencies. One of us had a wonderful relationship with a professor of statistics and met with this person during the analysis phase to confirm findings, choices of statistical treatments, and overall discussion of the merits and demerits of various analysis strategies. To say that these consultations were significant is an understatement; in fact, the professor wanted to attend the dissertation defense to add his support of the work that was done. Because he was a well-respected and well-known stats expert, the committee was assured of the reliability and validity of the data findings. (Yes, this is a CYA tactic.)

The warning bell that should be going off for you is that, regardless of who does the data work, you are responsible for the final analysis as well as full comprehension and understanding of the results and conclusions that you make. Many a committee member has caused havoc in a doctoral defense posing unanswerable questions about intricate statistical differences and what you should have considered. Your job is to be prepared, to know your data inside and out, and to know why you chose a specific statistical treatment as opposed to an alternate. You may even need to know—and mention—whose opinions you are following (yes, actual names of theorists you have followed) to present the best defense of your findings.

A final thought on the use of quantitative strategies is that these strategies rely on hard facts and numbers (a qualitative strategy relies on ideas and words). Quantitative methodologies manipulate variables and control natural phenomena. It is a process of deductive logic with a clear focus, objective data, controlled conditions, and valid results. A quantitative methodological strategy can be a clean, simple, and effective choice for your research if you have the support of your committee and if you have defined the important components and fully understand what they require: an obtrusive and controlled environment, objectivity, reliability, validity, stability, and generalizability. You'll need to accurately input your data and define the word *sample* as more than a simple taste of something.

Mixed Methodology
(aka The Servant of Two Masters)

You may be considering using a mixed methodological approach. All we can suggest is that you chase that idea out of your head ASAP. One of us did a mixed methodology in the dissertation and was so wrought with confusion and overload between the right and left sides of the brain that this strategy would not be recommended for anyone who wants to actually complete his or her dissertation before collecting social security.

The basic difficulty with a mixed strategy for your methodology is that you not only have to conduct two separate and distinct types of research, you have to write and write and research and research and analyze and analyze everything you do twice throughout your entire dissertation. This is not to say that some form of each methodology cannot be used, but the wise person will set limits prior to conducting the study. Don't kid yourself into thinking that two are better than one. Because most disciplines and fields favor one or the other methodological strategies, you as the researcher may not have the background or training to do a good job in the alternative methodology. Interplay of the research strategies may complicate your research and cause problems with the post-dissertation acceptance of the outcomes and results that will detract from the legitimacy and importance of your research. There are also expenses to consider when one chooses to use more than one methodology, and we would be quite naive to assume that doctoral students around the world are wealthy after paying the fees that most institutions assess for the privilege of adding three little letters after your name. Time is also a factor to consider. It will certainly take you more time to use two strategies.

Issues of methodology should be issues of strategy and not of moral value. The choice of a research strategy to be employed should result from a careful examination of the most meaningful and useful method(s) to the desired outcomes of the study. All strategies should be explored as alternatives early in your dissertation process, especially those involving your committee members' preferences and your college or school's preference and track record. Quantitative research cannot always answer the question of why. Qualitative research cannot always answer the question of what. Using both strategies may answer the questions of who, where, and when, but it may drive the doctoral student to bouts of anxiety, depression, and increased levels of frustration, drinking, and weight gain as she or he sits at the computer for hours and more hours analyzing data and trying to figure out how she or he is going to put an end to this self-induced madness.

In fairness to choosing a mixed methodological approach, the literature does support mixed strategies within certain investigative contexts. One can choose a separate but equal approach or an integrated approach. Separate but equal implies that different research strategies may be suitable for different types of research questions. When you are searching for meaning, a qualitative approach is more appropriate. When you are searching for distribution or correlation, a quantitative approach is more appropriate. Documented within your research proposal, you may want to use qualitative strategies such as interviewing to generate your hypotheses and quantitative strategies for testing of the hypotheses. In reverse, you may choose to conduct a survey (quantitative strategy) and then interpret or elaborate the results with qualitative (interviews) follow-up. Open-ended questions on a survey can be formulated to develop valid instruments for a later, larger scale study, or a survey instrument may be constructed from qualitative data that have been obtained from a small group.

An integrated approach implies triangulation (and, no, it's not part of the percussion family) or multiple operationism. This often involves combining different methods in the same research to reveal different dimensions of the same phenomenon, to strengthen shortcomings of each method, and/or to double-check findings by examining them from several different vantage points. The integration of different methods makes it possible to weave back and forth between different levels of meanings. One of the most acceptable ways to triangulate data includes document analysis or review within the context of a case study or naturalistic inquiry combined with the techniques to test a hypothesis or confirm or add to a significant finding in the more quantitative approach.

There are striking similarities that might lead one to think that researchers are not arguing against concepts between "quant." and "qual." as much as they may be arguing about styles and mindsets that have been established in the disciplines for a long period of time. All research findings should have results that actually answer the question(s) asked and data that are believable (either statistically or with the "makes sense" connotation). Two areas that seem in direct conflict with each other are objectivity versus subjectivity. Researchers are beginning to understand that no study collects completely neutral facts, that all research entails value decisions and to some degree reflects the researcher's selections, assumptions, and interpretations.

In choosing a mixed methodological approach, you acknowledge that your research has multiple purposes that warrant multiple approaches. Qualitative techniques could be defined as techniques of personal understanding, common sense, and introspection. Some examples are lifestyle issues such as postpartum depression, living with cancer, and working in cross-gender environments. Quantitative techniques could be defined as counting, scaling, and abstract reasoning, such as student opinion surveys, program evaluations, and genetic research. One cannot benefit from numbers alone if one doesn't understand what those numbers mean. Finally, by using methods of triangulation, biases that are present in every individual method may be corrected. The ultimate choice is about what fits your study, but remember that there is plenty of time in the future to mix methods, get paid for it, and get recognition for your efforts—something you will not have or get in the dissertation process.

A gender revelation is in order here: Qualitative research is not gender specific, although some will tell you it is. Qual. is done by men also. Real men do eat quiche. This seems a ridiculous section to even be writing in these times of striving for gender equity, but the reality is that qualitative research is not as well thought of by many in academia. Its roots are in the soft science fields such as anthropology, sociology, or psychology, and hard science field researchers find this against their beliefs that only hard, observable, factual, one-truth data exist. It's like people's religious beliefs and the concept of faith, believing in the unseen, the nonconcrete.

Within this context, males may feel that qualitative research is more female oriented, and that may truly be the case, except that the literature abounds with those of the male species who conduct qualitative research in all disciplines and fields of study. It would be tantamount to saying that all investigative reporters are male and females need not apply. We know the stereotypes but there is no need to perpetuate them. Having lived with the stereotypes for multiple centuries is enough.

What is needed for good qualitative research is curiosity, a propensity for listening rather than talking, creativity in getting to the question at hand, and a belief that people have multiple realities. It has never been expected that females could not conduct quantitative research, so the reverse also should not be expected. Those who are femininely challenged should not hesitate to create and design research with a qualitative strategy nor should either gender be forced into a methodological choice simply because of the side their shirts button on. The choice for a research strategy is individual and should be consistent with the research itself, its goals and outcomes, as well as the comfort level of the individual researcher in the technique that is to be used.

If you still have questions, a recommended reading list is included that has eight references to get you jump-started.

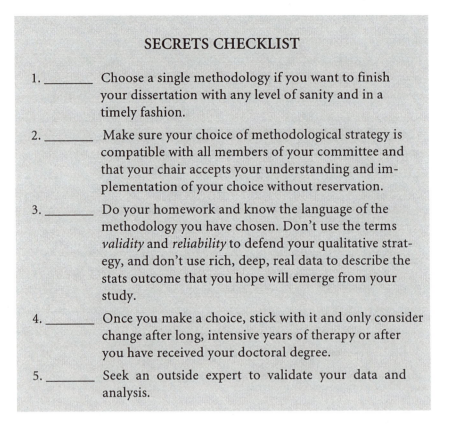

SECRETS CHECKLIST

1. _____ Choose a single methodology if you want to finish your dissertation with any level of sanity and in a timely fashion.

2. _____ Make sure your choice of methodological strategy is compatible with all members of your committee and that your chair accepts your understanding and implementation of your choice without reservation.

3. _____ Do your homework and know the language of the methodology you have chosen. Don't use the terms *validity* and *reliability* to defend your qualitative strategy, and don't use rich, deep, real data to describe the stats outcome that you hope will emerge from your study.

4. _____ Once you make a choice, stick with it and only consider change after long, intensive years of therapy or after you have received your doctoral degree.

5. _____ Seek an outside expert to validate your data and analysis.

3

Selecting Committee Members

(aka Animal Farm)

The selection of the dissertation committee members is the bumpiest decision that the doctoral student makes. All good (and we stress good) committee members will (and should) offer respect and support for the student. Research interests, previous working relationships, classroom teacher-student relationship, knowledge of methodology, writing, and editing skills should all be considered when selecting the committee. A supportive mentor is a good criterion for membership. A committee chair must be strong enough to protect you and your work when the going gets tough and at the same time must be critical when the work is not up to acceptable standards.

Most universities require that the committee include three or four members. Frankly, this is a time to realize George Orwell was right when he wrote, "All animals are equal, but some are more equal than others." (Do you suppose he was in a doctoral program when he penned those words?) A good committee enriches the areas of concentration by discussing ideas and methodologies. A combative, competitive, or just plain lousy committee will talk politics and tell jokes at your meetings, never addressing your issues and concerns. When you, the student, are positive that the topic and methodology are the best match, find a committee that will not only agree with your decision but also further encourage your ideas. Do not put someone on your committee who simply wants his or her own voice heard—you'll have enough voices to listen to. The purpose of a dissertation is to produce work in which the voice heard is yours as you represent your subjects and participants, or the findings represent strong, solid research strategies that produce valid and reliable data. The dissertation is not a reflection of your professors' opinions, no matter how loud their voices are. But also be aware that reality often interferes with the process; that is a fact of life.

One student suggested to each of us that we spend the necessary time to interview possible committee members with an air that these faculty members are fortunate even to be considered. In retrospect, we can agree. Students typically are a bit intimidated by professors because students lack the same status. However, a good dissertation topic should be interesting enough to attract the best committee.

If you find yourself having to select an "unknown" person as a committee member, do your homework. It is the student's responsibility to find someone who will provide an area of expertise that is needed, and there may not be anyone in the student's department who meets her needs. We know a doctoral student whose topic was intuition, and she wanted a committee member to guide her literature review and results. It was a difficult search.

One strategy is to ask for referrals from faculty, then read research and publications by these individuals. Another is to read dissertations on which they have served. An additional strategy may be to prepare a comprehensive working outline for the person's review. With your chair's permission, include your chair's phone number and encourage the prospective committee member to contact him or her with questions. Small courtesies, such as maps of your institution, locations and times of meetings, parking permits, and so on may sway the individual in your favor.

This process is riddled with angst. You may think you are asking a big favor of an individual when requesting him or her to serve on your committee. The truth is somewhat different. Faculty get recognition, status, and *compensation* (and that's an important word to remember) for serving on dissertation committees. Institutions that do not advise many dissertations have faculty that vie for that caveat to add to their tenure status. Being a member or chair of a doctoral dissertation committee is a bonus. Other institutions reward faculty with service time and credits for serving on a committee that they can turn in for nonclassroom teaching assignments. This, in theory, is in recognition of the time, effort, and support that is needed for a doctoral dissertation. Sometimes, for external members of a committee, there is a *stipend* payment (and that is also an important word for the candidate to remember) for service on a dissertation committee. A final word of warning here is that some faculty elect to serve on committees to further their own research efforts and their emphasis may be more self-serving than student-serving.

We recommend that you start at the top; first decide on your committee chair. Wait a week and if your decision is the same, ask that professor. With further input from the chair, you can complete the selection of the other committee members. Ask these new members and hope for the best. After the committee is formed, you will initiate meetings where four or five personalities must blend. Some students prefer working with their chair, only occasionally meeting with other committee members, and sending as few drafts as possible to the other members. Often, chairs prefer the same hierarchy. However you set it up, you will be spending significant time with these honored professors. Therefore, it is critical for everyone to understand their responsibilities and your expectations, and have the ability and desire to form a supportive group.

Even though all professors are professionals (well, they are supposed to be, but they are also people with opinions), you will find that professors prefer to work with some personalities and not others. Just as in other aspects of life, politics play an important role in this process, and students should know that they will not likely escape the politics of personality in their completion of the dissertation. To encourage an effective team, you should clarify your beliefs and discuss responsibilities immediately.

We highly recommend that each member be assigned or requested to perform specific tasks. One chair—and only one chair—one methodologist, and a third reader make a good committee. Clarify, at the beginning, who will be the methodologist on the committee. Several committee members may believe that they are the most competent in this area. Typically, there are disagreements as to acceptable methods used and therefore each member must have a clear understanding of which chapters she or he can influence. Other members should bite their tongues and wait for their specialty. However, we hear tales of faculty members making walls vibrate with their differing opinions. Faculty, like the student writing the dissertation, may exhibit strong convictions about any of the issues found in this process.

If necessary, put all assignments in writing so that you can refer to these agreements in case one committee member attempts to take control of another area of expertise. Who dictates the format? Who is first to read? Who is last to read? Who is disposable? You do not need to be tossed around more than necessary, and delegating responsibility at the beginning of the process alleviates further stress to the student as well as to the committee members. Some students begin this process as weaklings and feel they lack the strength to elaborate their concerns at the beginning. Those feelings will change as you are tossed around. The chances of making everyone 100% happy are between slim and none. Begin with strength and diplomacy. Learn the rules of the game and become a master of your own destiny. After all, you are paying, yes paying, for this privilege.

Reasons for Selecting Each Member
(aka Pride and Prejudice)

When choosing committee members, you want to carefully select professors who will readily agree that your ideal subject is a terrific original idea or will encourage another path with such enthusiasm that you, the student, remain committed to the dissertation process. You need to have confidence, but you also must listen to the member's advice. Isn't that why we have a committee in the first place? Therefore, you must remain open at all times, but also you must remain strong enough to fight for your beliefs even when the other committee members disagree with your opinion. Consider your committee's opinions before you react negatively. When you are sure you are on solid ground, fight for your opinion. If you won't fight for your own work, who will? We remember one student who had to fight for his methodology. This student was positive that no other method would adequately explore his subject, and because two of the committee members had not worked with this methodology before, they were skeptical. In the end, the student's methodology was accepted and all four of them added valuable information to their repertoires.

Just as all of us have our pride and the basic belief that we know what we are doing, we also have prejudice. Let's hope that by this time in your educational careers you can identify your prejudices and work within the constraints. Professors favor certain methodologies and certain subjects. You should consider these preferences when you make your selection. However, you will be better off if you fully comprehend going into this process that this is not the first priority of your committee. This is not going to be the Great American Historical Text, and this certainly is not something they take personally. It is a job. And we all know how we view our jobs, at times, and where we place our priorities.

You must be even stronger (perhaps even mind readers) to identify your committee's prejudices. For instance, some professors ignore their responsibility to the student to read the chapters in a timely manner. Some professors feel that their schedules are the most important aspect of their professional lives and are unwilling to make the slightest changes to accommodate a student's request, that is, to return a phone call within two days. A common frustration among doctoral students is the chronic "nonresponse" of some committee members. This occurs when chapters are submitted and follow-up phone calls are never answered. Others complain that appointments are missed or that ideas are dismissed with no explanation.

Let's face it, some professors have earned their "absent-minded" labels. Others are simply too flaky to remember your work from one conversation to another. If you are also a flake, then perhaps you can deal with unscheduled meetings, interrupted meetings, and postponed meetings. If, on the other hand, you are a student who has a strong obsessive-compulsive nature, and who lives by schedules, lists, and routines, then we advise you to find committee members who agree to a schedule in advance. There are marvelous and responsible professors out there who are like you and who will welcome meetings every other week or each month with chapter due dates clearly agreed upon.

Our personal feeling is that structure is necessary in this messy process. If the committee chair expects to see a chapter or revision on a certain date each month, that chapter has an increased likelihood of being completed and the dissertation should progress at a rapid pace. If, however, you are in no hurry to finish the degree, then no dates need be set, the dissertation will likely flounder, and you may graduate in the seven-year time allotment, or maybe not.

Scheduling is the ultimate responsibility of the doctoral candidate. It is critical that you do not rely on the method of "they will remind me." As one of our professors likes to remind students, "I am *not* your mother." It is not the professor's responsibility to remind you of schedules, so relying on yourself is the best advice we can give. Also, keep a sense of humor; you will need it through the tears of frustrations and the peaks and valleys as well as the troughs (discussed in Chapter 7) that you will experience.

Beware of Unreal Timetables
(aka Catcher in the Sky)

What would the ideal timetable look like? This is a difficult question because timetables will differ for each student. We would strongly recommend that you consider the timetable at the same time you are selecting your committee. Who does what when? The beginning of this process should be clarified in terms of the student's expectations as well as the committee members'.

Doctoral students need to be fair and to understand that the university "owns" this degree. Until the committee agrees to confer the degree on the doctoral candidate, students should not be in the mind-set that they are "owed" these final three letters. The requirements may occasionally push the student beyond his or her comfort zone, and this can be the source of many professor-student conflicts. Keep a note pasted above your computer: This is not the time for the "I'm Even Dumber Than I Originally Thought" Syndrome.

Stay in contact with your committee members so that they do not complain that you are suddenly demanding their time after long absences. If any member of the committee plans a sabbatical, then for how much time will that committee member be available? Some professors enjoy reading student dissertations during their sabbaticals because they have additional time to contemplate both problems and potential solutions in the dissertations. Other professors feel that their sabbatical is a long-awaited reward for their own reflection and research, and resent any student interference. If the former applies, appreciate your brilliance for placing that person on your committee. If the latter is the case, definitely discuss the possibility of replacing that member.

Our belief is that students should plan to write their dissertations within a year after the dissertation proposal defense. When students languish in their work longer than the one-year time frame, minor distractions may bloom into major obstacles. Relegating your dissertation to less than a number one priority only complicates the process. Write the proposal; defend the proposal. Spend a year writing the dissertation, then defend the dissertation. If you can complete the process faster, our hats are off to you. If you are slower, there should be significant reasons for the delay, such as having a baby, changing marital status, being bedridden from major surgery, or moving across the country. We know students who have done these things (not all at once) and still remained on their time schedules. Only you can decide what significant reason would slow your progress in finishing the last step in achieving your doctorate.

When to Replace a Chair
(aka For Whom the Bells Don't Toll)

The dissertation chair is like the traffic cop directing the intersection of people and ideas. What do you do when the chair you chose, the friend you confided and believed in, suddenly basks in newfound power and decides that the dissertation is relegated to the last task on his or her list? What about no response when work is turned in? What about the change in tone of comments such as, "You're bothering me with this slop? Go back to the drawing board and start over."

Well, it is time to start over. The first step is to select a new chair. Even if you have to redefend your proposal, now is the time to reposition yourself. If there are serious sparks at the beginning of the dissertation process, there will be major explosions as the process continues and you may never graduate. Remember the statistic that half (or more) of all students who begin doctoral programs never finish? So dump the problem professor at the beginning. It is far easier now than trying to get a committee chair or other member to resign later on.

How do you fire a chair? Gently, but with no wiggling around. Write a letter explaining the difficulties, but write with respect and choose your words carefully. Suggest that the member is far too busy to deal with your dissertation. Recognize that the member holds other more important responsibilities.

A sample letter might look like this, but please remember that each working relationship is unique and you'll have to write a letter for yourself:

Dear _____,

Thank you for your time, energy, editing, and helpful suggestions (or any other positives) in the development of my proposal. I deeply appreciate your support.

Several aspects of our working together have troubled me, however, and they are as follows (select those that apply):
_____ missed appointments
_____ nonresponse for submitted material
_____ lack of returned phone calls
_____ misplacing of materials I have submitted
_____ reluctance to schedule dissertation defense dates
_____ lack of communication with other committee members
_____ demanding sole decision making on all written work
_____ taking credit for my topic, my ideas, and my findings

I completely respect the fact that you
_____ are overworked
_____ are underpaid
_____ are deeply involved in your own research
_____ have medical problems
_____ are in the witness protection program and can't be located
_____ simply do not wish to work with me

Due to the above circumstances, I wish to relieve you of the responsibility of shepherding me through this final dissertation process.

I wish you luck, health, wisdom, and so on. Once again, many thanks for bringing me to this stage.

(Check the appropriate items)   Forever in your debt,
                                Respectfully yours,
                                With immense relief,
                                An Aspiring Doctoral Student

There is no need to express your secret belief that some professors are so self-absorbed that they haven't time to consider any work other than their own. Professors are people too and are dealing with their own challenges. But do be polite—one never knows about the later consequences of firing a member. Politics are both overt and covert at all universities, and there is no point in burning bridges.

Who Fixes Every Last Word?
(aka The Princess and the Pea)

No matter how competent you are, or how well you write, there are always differences in writing style. Some professors want to rewrite every sentence; others don't read carefully and simply want students to take full responsibility for their own work. Typically, a student has an idea of whether a professor approves of a student's writing style from class work during the doctoral program. However, the most supportive professor may suddenly become the most critical of the writing style during the dissertation process—an unwelcome surprise.

Another nightmare occurs when each draft is read by the other members and they disagree on the sentence structure. The chair may rewrite a sentence only to have another member rewrite it again, and then the third member may rewrite the sentence to be the same as the student originally had it or change it so much the meaning is lost. Needless to say, some students feel they are ready for an ambassadorial position at the end of their dissertations. One of our own solutions, and one that we all recommend, is to hire a professional editor, sending the revised copy with the invoice from the editor to all committee members. It helps (but is not necessary) if the editor has a Ph.D. in English!

Some committee chairs welcome a professional editor, and we feel this may be helpful to everyone. The student then does not have to convince the committee that the sentence is in fact structured correctly. If you can say the work has been through a professional editor, there is little recourse for a particularly compulsive professor who has no concept of time or closure. There are many editors working for publishing houses who enjoy reading dissertations on the side. Find a good one and invest the money if that makes your dissertation easier and ends your nightmares of demons or dragons.

If you elect not to use an editor, then who fixes every last word? We suggest you assign one professor to be the editor during the early stages of the process and make sure that the other members understand this assignment. Many professors will cheer the fact that they are not expected to do any editing and can focus on the methodology or the presentation of the material. They will still write notes in margins; it's impossible not to! Remember, the dissertation includes your ideas, your findings, your work, and your writing. If smaller details in the writing process can be simplified so you can graduate on your time line, go for it.

Over and Over Again (aka How It Is)

The student should remember that each committee member plays an important role. You will need to make decisions that can affect the rest of your life. And, yes, there is life after the dissertation! Think carefully about who can assist you in methodology without forcing his or her life views on you; think carefully who can assist you in organizing the content of your findings, who will challenge you to dig a bit deeper in your analysis. Think carefully about who can or may help you in the future, and about any political implications in what you are doing; think carefully about who really, really likes your style of writing and really, really likes you as a person; and, finally, think carefully about whom you do not want to spend those postdoctoral years hanging in effigy or cursing his or her children's children with voodoo chants.

Take the time to talk with and listen carefully to students who are already struggling with their committees; listen to the rumors (remember, where there is smoke, there is usually some kind of fire); and ask for opinions. The final, absolutely mandatory suggestion is that you find out about the process and procedure, both formal and between the lines, for changing (we won't say firing) any or all of your committee members and especially about changing your chair. You need to realize that, after all this work and all those tuition payments and all those late night classes, the dissertation process can make or break you. Your committee can be either your savior or your eulogizer. A good key to the success of your relationship with your committee can be gained at your proposal defense. If you feel uncomfortable and more anxious afterward, or if you continue to see red spots every time you focus your eyes or speak a person's name, then you need to examine why and look toward those reflections you are seeing. Even with all this, a lot can and does change between the proposal and the dissertation defense.

Some professors are intent on upholding the ivory tower academic standards in subtle ways—a level that some students may want to distance themselves from because of a need to graduate and find a job. Here are some indicators that there is trouble in paradise:

1. Your chair says to other committee members and friends who have joined you for your proposal defense, "I don't think you are ready. We will have to cancel this defense and ask the audience to leave at this time."

2. A committee member says, "Oh, well, what difference does it make *when* you graduate?"

3. Your chair says, "You can't defend this next month, you haven't contacted me in over four months," and you have proof of phone calls.

4. A committee member says, "Oh, yes, and you are ???"

5. Your chair says, "You haven't spent enough time in this program. No, you can't defend and graduate that soon."

If you think these aren't real issues, you will need to reassess your thoughts about those who walk in hallowed halls. And you think we made these up? All of the above happened to people we know.

SECRETS CHECKLIST

1. _____ Before choosing a committee, check with students who have been there, done that.

2. _____ Choose your committee chair, wait a week, and then ask the professor.

3. _____ Meet with the chair and come to an agreement about the other two members.

4. _____ Ask these new members and hope for the best.

5. _____ Assign responsibilities for each committee member during a group meeting so that all issues are clarified.

6. _____ Put the dissertation's timetable in writing.

7. _____ If the process is not moving along as expected, take necessary action.

8. _____ Hire an editor.

9. _____ Exercise regularly and maintain a sense of humor.

4

Surviving the Human Subjects Committee

(aka Of Human Bondage)

Universities have committees to review faculty and student research in the hopes of avoiding dangerous human landslides. The purpose of the Committee on the Protection of Human Subjects (CPHS or any other title the university chooses) is to examine several components of all research so that any and all subjects are protected from harm by eliminating, reducing, or managing research risks. Remember, federal and institutional requirements must be met before research has begun. Students cannot break these rules. You are like the man Phaedo spoke of when he said, "Man is a prisoner who has no right to open the door of his prison and run away."

This committee reviews the research design to ascertain the validity of the chosen method. Of course the competency of the researcher is also considered as well as any consequences that the research may have upon human life. The selection of the subjects and/or participants is important to the committee as well as voluntary consent. Participants or subjects should be advised that they are participating in research. No one should be forced to participate in any research. Subjects have the right not to participate and to withdraw from a study at any time during the research. All matters concerning compensation are stated in the submission form that is given to the Human Subjects Committee or CPHS.

Some dissertations do not need approval from the Committee on the Protection of Human Subjects. For instance, if you are writing a historical study concerning Houdini, you will not be able to interview him unless you have contacts unrecognized by the scientific community. Obviously, you will not need CPHS approval. If, however, you plan to interview living persons, experiment on living persons, or have personal contact with any supposedly alive persons as a part of your dissertation, then you need to submit a proposal to the Human Subjects Committee before you even think of beginning your study. This chapter is for those persons who will have contact with other persons in the process of obtaining their data.

Playing by the Rules
(aka Lords of Discipline)

We strongly urge that you not submit your proposal to use human subjects until after your successful dissertation proposal defense. Your dissertation committee may suggest changes that you failed to anticipate, and if you had previously submitted your work to the CPHS, then you would have to resubmit it. If you successfully defend your proposal (which will be no problem after reading Chapter 1), then you are ready to jump through the next hoop—approval of your study from the Committee on the Protection of Human Subjects.

The proposal at this time will include any changes that your committee requests. You may have to rewrite the proposal to reflect these changes but, remember, better now than next month. After these changes are made and you have the blessing of your committee chair, it is time to approach the Human Subjects Committee. You must have the committee's approval before the study begins. Don't think you can fool anyone here. Do not begin the research until you have the human subjects permission form signed. If you begin before their OK, they may shove your research into a black hole for all eternity.

The preparation of your human subjects proposal will, in most cases, be "cut-and-paste" pieces from your original and now-revised defense proposal. There will be some specific areas to address and most Committees for the Protection of Human Subjects outline these in printed instructions. CPHS committees are sometimes made up of representatives from all faculties and a representative of students within the institutions, and some are made up of full-time appointed positions. They may or may not be familiar with your topic, but their job is to protect you, your subjects, and the university from making blunderous errors as well as preventing costly lawsuits.

Members of the Committee for the Protection of Human Subjects take their jobs very seriously, but they also take their commitments to students and research just as seriously. Remember, they are not the enemy. Don't feel you have the right of editorial opinion here; if something does not apply that CPHS has listed, tell them in your proposal. If something does apply, give them enough information to make a fair and just decision. Fill out the forms or documents as completely as possible. There are actual horror stories of students not taking this stage seriously and thoughtfully, and having to abandon their original research and actually begin anew. Think of this process as the part of the journey that ensures you are on the right track and not getting off the train in Detroit when you should be in Chicago. If, and that is a big if, something should go wrong during your research, Human Subjects Committees will be part of your defense if you have complied with their guidelines and stayed true to your research objectives and plans.

There are typically two types of proposal requests. The first, those proposals seeking an expedited review, do not include serious risk to the population you are studying. This type of study includes interviewing participants as to their thoughts on a given subject where there is no likelihood of inflicting physical or psychological harm.

Research studies that involve the collection of survey data, descriptive data, including collection of baseline data, and even some short-answer questions may also be approved through an expedited review. There is beauty and expediency in anonymity (most surveys are anonymous, thus affording great protection from harm). Blind studies and studies involving treatments, even the use of placebos, may require more detailed information. If you are going to test the latest flavors of Häagen-Dazs ice cream, you may want to ask about allergies to any animals, minerals, or vegetables.

Some institutions have selected faculty in the various disciplines to serve as ex officio members of the Committee for the Protection of Human Subjects. Their job, as a first step, is to recommend your research for expedited review to the CPHS chair. This is the first level to talk with if you have any concerns or are unsure of your proposal's status. If such a person does not exist, call the chair of the CPHS after you talk with your own chair. Remember, your dissertation committee chair must be informed of any and all changes. This expedited process is typically faster than a full review and should be used when you have the proper type of study.

When there is the possibility of risk to a participant in the study, one applies for a full review, the second category. Full reviews are typically done when there are risks to any of the following populations: fetuses, pregnant women, prisoners, and/or children. Your university may include other populations such as the aged, minorities, or the disadvantaged, so check with your committee and understand their requirements.

There are basically three types of risk in research. Physical harm usually involves medical procedures. However, injury due to physical activities and health concerns are also possibilities. Psychological risk can occur when researchers investigate particularly sensitive issues that require the subject or participant to consider the consequences of some action that may not have been brought to the forefront before, or that the subject now recognizes as more serious than previously considered. The third form of risk in research involves social or economic risk. Knowledge of drug abuse, illegal activities, and mental illness can all be devastating to any person if confidentiality is lost. Future employment, social standing in the community, and criminal prosecution are all possibilities. Confidentiality in this type of research is paramount.

You may have heard horror stories about the Human Subjects Committee at your university. We are proud to say that none of us had any problems getting our dissertations through this group, but we were careful with our submissions. First, learn the rules of the committee. They have deadlines and they do not like exceptions. If you fail with the simple rules, watch out. Remember, they have the final say about your study and their memories may be longer than you think or fear.

If the committee meets every month, find out the last possible date for consideration of your proposal for that meeting and make sure your research proposal is submitted several days prior to that date. Now is the time for your obsessive-compulsive nature to leap out and take over. Make sure you have completed all the appropriate forms, checked the correct boxes, and made the necessary number of copies. Any nonpublished measurement instruments must also be included. If you are going to ask your subjects a list of questions or give them a questionnaire to fill out, submit a copy with your proposal. The purpose of the committee is to protect all human subjects from unnecessary risk, and you the student must demonstrate that you are not going to stick pins in your subjects or conduct exorcism rites unless you have a valid reason and can stipulate that the risk is outweighed by the potential benefits of the study.

Second, carefully consider your research methodology. Does it match your purpose and population? Not only does the committee examine the possibility of risk to the study population, they also will consider the methodology the researcher has selected as well as the purpose of the study. Therefore, the proposal should include the background of the issue, statement of purpose, general information concerning the methodology, research design (specific characteristics of the study such as time limits of the study and the handling of data), questions the researcher will ask of the participants, makeup of the target population, how they will be selected as well as the site, how subjects will be protected from unnecessary risk, treatment protocols, limitations of the study, and appendixes that include the consent form and copies of any correspondence you have with your subjects.

Third, references are a necessary part of this process. Cite many refereed journals and skip best-seller lists. Popular magazines have their place in our lives but should not dominate any research proposals. Consider your professional/educational background. The type of citations indicate to the Human Subjects Committee the depth of your research. Citing current pop psych articles on chaos theory as it relates to criminal behavior is not satisfactory. So use common sense and remember that the people serving on the Committee for the Protection of Human Subjects have varied backgrounds and someone will have some familiarity with your topic. Typically, they will recognize the referenced journals and authors. "Cute" is out; thoroughness rules.

Intentions (aka You Just Don't Understand)

The committee cannot assume that you are a qualified person to attempt any study and therefore it is up to you to give enough information so that there will be an acceptable conclusion to this process. We know you have common sense; now is the time to haul it out. Do you have the qualifications to perform the study? For instance, if you have no prior training in human behavior, interviewing participants about thoughts of suicide may trigger emotional upheavals that you do not have the knowledge to deal with—that's putting your subjects at risk. If your background is in engineering, do you have the skills to interview violent criminals about their thoughts at the time they committed their crimes? Be open and honest about your intentions. But, remember, do not state requirements that you cannot successfully meet.

Also recognize that your study may need to be modified. If you do not want to return to the Committee for the Protection of Human Subjects for another approval, then leave little detail out of the proposal. When we state "little detail," we mean just that. You may not be able to begin your study on April 1 and end March 31 so don't be that specific. However, don't state that you will begin your study two weeks after final approval of your topic and then begin two days before approval is received. Remember, those committee members are accepting your word as truth. You do need to state the study's approximate duration and each student's length of participation.

Let's face it, in any research there is some risk. Risk is often limited to the possibility of minor fatigue during a possible lengthy interviewing process or a commitment of time for a treatment or a syndrome of a participant observitis (similar to microscoptitis but not fatal) although some students claim that "terminal boredom" is also a factor. However, some studies will include risk to the study's population. If there is any risk at all, state it. All participants/subjects have the right to be informed. When there is risk, what will the risk management procedures be? State them also.

If the research is valid, there will be benefits. What are the benefits? You might have the overwhelming desire to claim that your project is at the cutting edge of all future knowledge and all society will benefit, but you must be realistic—even humble. Consider the possible benefits of the study. If your mind comes up blank, move to another idea.

Are you going to pay your subjects/participants? State that there is payment "in the amount of ___ " or that there will be no payment. Ideally, your participants will feel so fortunate that they were chosen and so excited to share their life stories and knowledgeable opinions that they will not expect any payment and may even offer to pay you so that they will hold your undivided attention. There are ethical data collection methods and assessments. You will want numerous refereed journals to contact you at the end of this massive work, so remain ethical at all times.

Anytime a researcher is interviewing someone, there must be a signed consent form. The researcher should identify him- or herself and position at the university on this form such as Janque Right, a doctoral candidate at the University of Curiosity, North Southern. Also included on this form should be specified the intention of the study, how many times you will meet, the length of each encounter, if and why phone conversations may be added, the use of tape recordings and transcriptions, who has permission to edit, any payments for participation, participation and risk, confidentiality, voluntary participation, and the researcher's name and number where he or she may be reached.

How Not to Hang Yourself (aka The Rope)

The following are some areas where students tend to slip up and the committee will require revisions:

1. When a researcher is interviewing children, parental or guardian permission must be sought. The research should also consider the age of the child and decide whether the minor should also sign a permission form. For example, most 15-year-olds are capable of making a decision as to their participation. Even though the law may require that the parent sign a consent form, the researcher may also want the child to sign one.

2. If the interviews are tape-recorded and anonymity is promised, how are the tapes going to be protected? Where will they be stored? Will they be destroyed at a stated time? Will any and all identifiable information be erased from the tapes? Will the researcher promise confidentiality and then sneak all the tapes to *Hard Copy* for a nice profit?

3. If the interviews are taking place at a specific site or the researcher is using people and labs at Western Research Institute, then a site supervisor or representative from the location needs to submit a signed letter to the Human Subjects Committee stating that agreement.

4. Students often fail to identify the specific methods used to protect anonymity or confidentiality. Will there be pseudonyms used on the final copy?

5. State on the consent form that the participant or subject has the right to withdraw from the study at any time. The possibility of a participant dropping out is admittedly highly unlikely if you, as a researcher, have prepared your study well.

6. Is the researcher going to offer psychological counseling if the topic is so upsetting that the participant feels like jumping off London Bridge after the interview?

7. The researcher must use his or her name and phone number on the consent form. If the participants need to reach said researcher at 3:30 a.m., they should have the right to do so. That is the chance the researcher takes when selecting his or her participants, whether in qualitative or quantitative studies.

All of the above might appear to be overwhelming but, like all other challenges, the best style is to break it into small chunks. Just take one paragraph at a time and make sure that each condition is met. If you can follow all of the above steps, your human subjects approval will be granted immediately.

SECRETS CHECKLIST

1. _____ Check the regulations of the Human Subjects Committee at your university.

2. _____ Play by the rules by meeting all deadlines.

3. _____ Concentrate on refereed journals and highly regarded books.

4. _____ Carefully consider all risks your participants or subjects will encounter.

5. _____ Human Subjects Committee members have long memories. When changes are suggested, take them seriously.

5

Collecting Data

(aka Far From the Maddening Crowd)

This can turn out to be a big, perilous topic, and because it is the crux of your dissertation, we have separated the chapter into two sections to address it more thoroughly, covering both the art of interviewing and building survey instruments. Please remember, however, that regardless of your method of collecting data, there will be times when you may be tempted to misquote Ogden Nash, whining, "I feel like I'm in the Land of Oz, just trying to tell it like it was." This is a normal stage, but it will be the only misquote you will be allowed to make in the entire process.

If you are doing a purely quantitative project, preferring anonymous charts of numerical calculations to real live people (biases do appear, you know, in both forms of research), then you may want to skip this first part of the chapter. Pass at your own risk, however, because both sections deal with information gathering, analyzing results, and drawing your conclusions. Those of you in what is commonly known as the "hard" sciences, who need every-thing proven 10 times over and seen and heard and tasted and touched to be believed, don't require strong interview skills for your research. You can't get much information out of a mouse, or an atom, or a virus, or the corpus callosum, by talking to it. You may not even get much out of a quantitative-minded colleague.

But many investigators of human behavior are now choosing the path of Real People Research, as some qualitative researchers like to call it, which has vastly improved the research environment for people who would like to better understand the lives and expe-riences shared by ordinary people. No charts or percentages or tight-fitting boxes here—just lots of flexibility for interesting ad-ventures. Gathering stories and information and impressions and emotions—all the good gooey stuff that makes up everyone's daily lives—is the heart of qualitative research. To gather this informa-tion, the researcher needs two basic skills: the ability to formulate informative questions and the ability to listen—mostly the latter, but many researchers get mixed up and concentrate on the former.

A talker is not an interviewer, but a listener is. And that's the only secret to being a good interviewer: Listen. Don't interrupt, don't change the subject, don't answer questions for the inter-viewees, and don't try to put words in their mouths. How can you possibly know what is floating around in another person's skull? What good is your research if you glue your words and impressions onto your subject's thoughts? Listen. Guide the conversation, if you must, to stay near the subject, but be brief and then just listen.

Tape Talk (aka Confessions of a Justified Sinner)

The following is equipment you simply cannot do without (trust us, we tried):

1. The *tape recorder* should be small, easy to run but *not* with a voice-activated switch that eliminates pauses in normal speech

patterns. Check the quality of the microphone to see if you prefer a portable mike with a cord.

2. Splurge on the purchase of *extra tapes and batteries* to carry with you, as the peace of mind definitely balances the minor cost. Also consider that experienced (aka compulsive) interviewers often carry around a second tape recorder as a backup.

3. The *tape transcribing machine* should have earphones and speed control. You may be able to borrow this machine but it may not be available when you need it. If you have extensive interviews, or plan to take your time, you might as well invest in your own machine. Make sure the transcriber takes the same size tapes that fit in your tape recorder.

4. *Note pads and pens* for field notes can be of any size or kind you prefer.

Now you are ready to conduct interviews—almost.

Be Prepared (aka Get Thee
to the Appointment)

Take a few moments to practice pushing the buttons on your tape recorder so you know what sound it makes when the first side runs out and you need to quickly flip over the tape, so you know which lights turn on/off when recording, and so you are familiar with its quirks. We also suggest you set the tape at the beginning, then record your name, the date, the time and place of the interview, and the interviewee's name, if you desire. Play it back to make sure everything works, then quickly jam down the stop button at the end of that information. You are now ready to record your interview.

Also, carry the cord with you and plug in the tape recorder when possible to save your battery juice. (Of course, you still would carry extra batteries in your bag; we know you are smart enough for that trick.) Many times you will not have an electrical outlet handy, but when you do, use it to save some wear and tear on your equipment as well as your panic mode.

You also will have a complete list of questions prepared, as this was submitted in your proposal defense. Many researchers begin with a solid, short list of questions; this can range from one question, in a phenomenological study, to three or four for a narrative, to hundreds of general questions for a case study or ethnography. Even one question can lead in many directions, so keep an open mind. Also include a list of ideas to spark conversation. Two additional papers would include a list of phone numbers (in case you get lost on the way to the interview and need directions) and the consent form, which must be signed before the interview begins.

If the participant's responses ramble far afield, you may be smart to let 'em do so. Participants often need some "warm-up" time to get to the heart of questions. You'll probably get the best information of the entire interview in the last few minutes when the individual tries to cram all the last pearls into the session. When you turn off the tape recorder, stay alert—either have a backup tape recorder running to catch those powerful last words or simply turn the first recorder back on. Forget your own personal time schedule and hunger pangs; if you have a hot subject, eager to talk, let him or her roll. You'll be glad you did.

Interview Challenges
(aka Three Horse-People of the Apocalypse)

We have run into several interesting groups of subjects in our experiences as students, teachers, newspaper writers, professors, project directors, counselors, dissertation interviewers, and women who seem to elicit life stories (even in the grocery store) without even trying. At the risk of being accused of generalizing (the most common put-down by the occasional stuffy quantitative folks for us down-to-earth qualitative-minded folks), we boldly chose to discuss three types of people you are likely to encounter. You will find many more, of course, but this is a start.

The Dust Bowl

This participant will not talk. If she or he does venture a word or two, it is as dry and tasteless as Oklahoma in the 1880s. The only words Dust Bowls are comfortable with are their own names, and even those may be mumbled. You might want to loosen them up by having them repeat their vital statistics even though you already have that information from your preliminary consent form. When you move to the important questions, however, you still may get nothing in response.

The expensive books tell you, as the interviewer, to ask "open-ended questions," questions that cannot be answered by a simple yes or no. The books are basically right, but even a Dust Bowl can find a creative shortcut for an answer. For example:

Interviewer: "Tell me about your childhood."
Participant: "OK."

Silence.

Interviewer: "Please share with me some events from your childhood."
Participant: "Uh, don't remember much." Or, "Only child, what's to say?"

Or the capper from the participant, "What do you want to know?" which throws the interviewer backward into yes-no questions again. This qualifies as a true Maalox Moment. But we always try again. It's our job.

So, what do you do with a Dust Bowl? Do you stick around and try to beg for snippets of information that will add depth and dimension to your research? Or do you say thank you and move quickly to the next participant on your list? We say move on. Dust Bowls rarely offer fountains of flowers bursting with interesting thoughts. If you are interviewing in a group setting, try to separate the Dust Bowls from the others—that monosyllabic stuff is contagious. You won't graduate if all you do is suck up dust.

The Avalanche

Ahhh, here we have the opposite problem. Avalanches are the participants who act so excited to be interviewed, and so thrilled at the sound of their own voices, that their words tumble all around you in an indecipherable mass of sounds.

Interviewer: "Tell me about your experiences as a special ed teacher."
Participant: "Oh, it's been so, the kids are really, and I never have
seen such wonderful, this one student, so adorable,
all those curly-headed, oh, can't believe what he
brought to class yesterday, I've had to choke back
tears so many, and then the principal gave me this
new, and we've all learned about, oh dear, I should
tell you about Johnny, he has the most fascinating
little . . . uh, what was your question again?"

The Avalanche presents a challenging interview, but if you can nudge the participant to stay on track on one subject, and make your questions specific, you often can gather a great deal of information. Some of it may even be useful. These enthusiastic interviewees tend not to censor any thoughts or feelings, thus yielding much valuable information, but they also tend to exhaust and confuse you. If you are the type of person who can find kernels in all this chaff, you'll survive everything the Avalanches throw at you and be ready for the next one. Tape recorders are indispensable.

Frankensteins

This is one of the early-stage nightmares we all seem to have before venturing forth to our first interview. What if everything goes wrong? What if the person is so off the wall that I feel like I'm in another world? What if the tape recorder breaks, or the tape runs out and I don't know when to turn it over? What if I forget to bring my list of questions? What if we get interrupted 15 times and none of it makes any sense? What if the person turns out to be someone else entirely and I don't even have the savvy to figure it out? What if this person gets angry or upset with me, what should I do? What if he or she cries? What if he or she walks out on me? What if he or she throws things?

What if, what if, what if? We can all create Frankenstein nightmares if we allow them into our world—but a few commonsense rules of organization and preparation should hold the monsters at bay. Keep your interviewing equipment well organized: the tape recorder, pens, paper, extra batteries and cord, additional blank tapes, and your list of questions tucked into a bag and left intact, ready to travel to each site. No sense making yourself a nervous wreck by double- and triple-checking it each time; just pick it up and haul it off to your interviews. You can add gum or aspirin or tranquilizers or chocolate if you need confidence boosters, but basically the ingredients should remain the same. If you don't have that magic bag ready, one of your key interviewees will call you in a panic and reschedule that precious interview to right now because he is going out of town on an emergency cruise. So be ready to grab the equipment bag and be out the door in a well-organized flash. End of first nightmare.

What if the person ends up to be someone other than the one scheduled or has completely misrepresented his or her position? Are you going to say, "Jeez, you're the wrong person!" and bolt from the room? Maybe. But we hope you are professional enough to stay and complete the interview. It's good practice and you may discover a hidden world of information never dreamed of in your planning. You may also spend the most boring or uneventful interview of your entire project, but how do you know that this won't lead to something even better? If you have the attitude that there are no coincidences, that everything leads to something else, then you'll keep your confidence and skills working smoothly. Flexibility brings an end to this second nightmare.

The third Frankenstein is a personality clash so full of lightning and thunder that no matter what you say or do, it simply will not be a positive experience. But positive vibes are not required for the gathering of information, and you cannot hope to make a terrific contact with everyone you encounter. Salvage as much of the interview as you can and look at it as a learning experience. (One of our colleagues spoke of these interviews as "character-building" events, but then announced, halfway through a long and difficult interviewing process, "I now have overflowing buckets of character and I don't need any more!") The end of this nightmare is the end of the interview process.

What Now? (aka I Can't Believe They Said That)

You may now be prepared for the caricatures you may find in interviewing, but you also need to be prepared for the characters or context of the interview. In qualitative research, you are searching for something—a lived experience, a description of a phenomenon, a common voice trying to be heard, the meaning of words or phrases, or patterns, themes, and commonalities. Don't be surprised if after your first interview you question what you were thinking when you contemplated undertaking this process.

This syndrome, known as "I Can't Believe They Said That and How Does It Apply?" also known as "Oh My God What Will I Do With This Crap?" often persists throughout the first series of interviews. Do not throw in the towel. Give yourself time to soak up what the words meant, to think through what you have discovered, what you've heard, what you've seen, and what you've felt. You may discover that what you thought was a dry mine turns out to be the Mother Lode of all information. It will take hours of transcribing, hours of listening to your tapes until you can repeat them verbatim, and it will take even more hours if what you hear and see disagrees with your preconceived convictions. Remember, you proposed that your data would emerge. This is qualitative research, remember?

People do not use the exact same words to express their beliefs, feelings, attitudes, or thinking. If you paid attention in your qualitative research class and you did the practice assignments, you will realize that time is your best ally. It is your job to pull together the overarching ideas and concepts, and you will. With time and study and reflection, you will be able to conjoin abstracts among your interviews—and the more interviews, the easier this will become, and the faster your nervous stomach will return to its normal size and functioning.

Qualitative strategies do work and they can work beautifully if you remember that you are the instrument, you are the "treatment," you are the analysis strategy, and you chose to conduct qualitative research. You may even have thought it would be easier than statistics. Some joke, eh?

The Concreteness of Surveys (aka No Names)

A great deal of research is conducted by using surveys instead of personal interviews, but because you are still gathering information about people, and their ideas, opinions, and feelings, this is the logical place for this discussion.

If your research involves a pure and simple survey to collect your data, or to gain baseline data, or for any other data purposes, then you now have the "Paper and Pencil" Syndrome. This syndrome often inundates one with symptoms of validity, for all of the face, content, internal, and external varieties. You will also notice validity's nasty twin sister of reliability sneaking into your pure and simple survey. To further complicate the syndrome, you now have somewhat hidden manifestations of double-barreled, "ambiguitive," open-ended "questionitis," and of course the ill-fated number one intimidating symptom called "return rate." These are common enough for all who enter the survey landscape, and although they add bumps along the road, some mortality, and some insignificance, your findings may still be salvageable.

If you still are a believer in a pure and simple survey, then you will need to take those few precious dollars you have left after paying tuition to beg, borrow, or copy books that tell you how, why, when, what, and where surveys can and do go wrong. These range from the simplistic versions *Surveys for Dummies* to the absurd *Quantitative Data Collection Analysis: The Hard Way*. This is one area that can and will haunt you through your entire dissertation process, particularly if you put a stats member on your committee. If you can't join in gleeful repartee about correlation, post hoc findings, a secondary hypothesis, interaction effects, and the pros and cons of factor analysis, then you do still believe in Santa Claus and the Tooth Fairy.

There are two ways to go with surveys and questionnaires. The first is to replicate or use an already established survey or questionnaire. In this case, one is wise to get the actual test manual and all that small, illegible print that outlines the methodological strategy, the validity and reliability of the survey administrations, as well as critiques and criticisms of that particular instrument. There is a book by O. K. Buros, available in most libraries that has compiled what others in the field say about nationally recognized testing instruments. Take the time to dig into what has been said by whom, under what circumstances, and when. It will come into play in the section named "Limitations" and will also give you a fair amount of ammunition when your stats committee member comes after you with guns blazing. Also remember that if you are using a published instrument, you will have to get permission from the publishers; most are copyrighted and you as an honest, hard-working, ethical, and moral student know the perils of using copyrighted materials without permission.

The problem with already published instruments is that they often don't meet very individual needs or situations that you may already have outlined. If you find that your specifics and the actual instrument as it stands have words, phrases, or areas that just don't fit your situation, these can usually be amended. But, again, you need to reread the above paragraph because even amendments need all the rest of the procedural steps that have been outlined. If you now have decided that your only hope is to design your own survey or questionnaire, welcome to the world of Survey Nightmare on Elm Street.

Survey and Questionnaire Decisions (aka The Good Soldier)

The first decision you will most likely make is which demographic categories you will use or need to collect given your methodology. It won't work if you have chosen an analysis of variance, designed your 60-question Likert scale survey, and decided not to collect demographic information or categorical variable data. Sounds ridiculous, but it happens. Also, any demographic question you construct may have implications in your literature review. If you ask the question of sex: ___male; ___female; you will need to discuss why this variable has any relationship to your topic. Yes, that means you will be adding another section to your literature review.

The same is true with demographic information that asks for age, job or level of job, educational background—in fact, just about anything. Also remember that once you collect this type of data, you will have to report it in your findings section, usually in Chapter Four. Some dissertation writers think that this type of data is extraneous, but it is the only way to define your population sample and allow you to talk about external validity, and your committee, especially that pesky stats person, will look for it.

A final hint about the actual design of your survey. Make it look like a survey. We all know what one looks like: lots of questions—fill in, check one, circle the best answer, and so on. A survey is a survey is a survey and by any other name they all look the same. Your participants expect a survey that has good face validity, not one that looks like a connect-the-dot coloring book exercise. With the use of computer graphic programs, this is a task that even the average computer user can accomplish. If you want people to check only one response, you need to tell them that; if you want people to circle only one number, you need to be quite explicit in your instructions. You can use arrows or notes to ask people to be sure to turn the page over or to proceed to the next page. It is really disheartening if half of your surveys that you designed as a front-to-back instrument come back with only the front page completed.

If you want to collect age information, it is best to use categories or ranges. For some reason, we all feel better with a range than specifics (this is usually if you fall into the upper ranges of the age levels; getting older is not something most people like to brag about, and many of them are quite adept at shaving years). The use of various ranking scales and such for certain items also needs explicit directions. If you have asked participants to rate something from 1 to 10, let them know that there really are no "ties" and you can't use the half number to rate their choices.

Pilot Studies/Identified Population (aka The Rehearsal)

Another little secret is to know the members of your population. It does no good to use a Likert scale with designations of "totally disagree, somewhat disagree, neutral, somewhat agree, and totally agree" if you are surveying third graders on their opinions of a physical education program. In this case, speak with the third-grade teachers on what would work best. A doctoral student faced with this dilemma ended up reading the questions to the students and designed his scale in various stages of "smiley-frowning" faces. (He found this idea during his Review of Literature.) He also had all the choices posted on a large piece of paper on the blackboard as he administered his survey.

As your survey is being designed, you will need to address the issues of content and face validity. This could and should include a pilot study. The purpose is not to find out the differences between American, United, Alaska, and Delta pilots and their preferences for flight attendants; the purpose is to "test" your survey. Find someone who can give you constructive feedback on the words you have chosen in designing your questions, the amount of time it takes to complete the survey, and if there are any confusing instructions or questions and directions that are not clear. If your pilot study includes people who may have knowledge of your topic, this is even better because they can make suggestions, and they will, very strongly, if you have not covered the content of the topic. Remember that you, as the researcher, take all comments resulting from a pilot study under consideration and, in your best judgment, you decide if you want to make a revision. It also gives you great text to use in your methodology chapter, which just happens to include a section on the pilot study.

In deciding about the administration of the survey or questionnaire, consider the types of populations you are dealing with. You know the old saying: If you want something done right, do it yourself. There is a lot of common sense here if it can fit into your methodology and your population is accessible. Relying on others to administer your instrument with the care and concern and thoroughness that you need is a matter of great trust. If you have lots of best friends that can and will work with you, then you are in great shape. If you are relying on people you don't know very well, you may have to go to Plan Two.

Plan Two still involves personal contact but it may be in the form of a phone call, an invitation to coffee, or gaining the support of management within the organization to stress the importance of completing the survey. Play politics here and don't get your population upset by your strategies. One doctoral student used her connections with local superintendents to be sure her survey was answered by teachers. At the next mandatory in-service teacher workshop, the superintendent required participants to remain after the all-day workshop for about 30 minutes to complete the survey. One participant was so angered by this that he called the student's university graduate division and complained about the student's use of this strategy to guarantee her return rate. Bottom line: Complete your research ethically, which means without pulling rank.

If your population is so diverse that you have to rely on the snail mail system, there are a few little secrets to remember here. Mailed survey return rates are not going to be high; people just don't give a survey their first priority regardless of how well it is designed. Setting a time limit for returns in two weeks will only make you more anxious and disappointed when 5 of your 500 surveys are returned to you, even though you enclosed self-addressed stamped envelopes.

One doctoral student we know tried a mail survey to students who had dropped out of school. He was amazed that he only received 3 surveys out of 150 sent out; 35% of his surveys were returned stamped "addressee unknown." He finally resorted to a more qualitative approach and conducted telephone or personal interviews with 30 carefully selected and available students who had dropped out of school. The moral of this story is that if you insist on a mail survey, you will certainly have to buy stamps and plan on a second mailing with a friendly reminder, a second stamped return envelope enclosed, and a second copy of the instrument with a second deadline date. Two mailings are usually enough to satisfy committee members and your academic committee. Remember that statistics don't mean much if 70% of your completed surveys indicated males and 30% indicated females and only 10 people returned the surveys. It is hard to determine any long-lasting and valid conclusions based on this type of data.

Although surveys generally are anonymous and confidential, if your population sample contains groups that you want to compare, you may want to code your return envelopes or color code your surveys so that you can determine who actually responded with a completed survey. Numbering surveys has been used but many respondents are cognizant of this strategy and either blacken out or actually tear off the number of the survey or just simply won't complete the survey as requested. Are there little secrets here to assist in a good return rate? Not really, but if you are open and honest and up front in your cover letter or instructions, most people will understand and, we hope, return your survey. Check with your methodology person on your committee prior to distribution if you are concerned with this area.

Types of Surveys to Expect (aka Specimen Days)

As with the art of interviewing section earlier in this chapter, there are also several interesting groups of subjects who will respond to your request for their opinions. Here is a hint of the three most common members of the survey response species.

The Noncommitted

These respondents will circle or indicate all neutral or mid-range numbers when they are faced with making a decision on a Likert scale. It's hard to know if they actually don't have an opinion, are trying to make a point to you that they are sick and tired of filling out surveys, or if number three is their favorite number and they like putting circles around it. There isn't much you can do unless you see this happen to a lot of your surveys. In this case, you may have chosen the wrong sample for your population or you have actually found something that people just don't care about enough to take a definite stand on. This can be an important finding in some cases but it causes havoc to those bar graphs or pie charts or categorical frequency distributions that you were planning to use to display your data.

The Minimalist

This type of respondent will complete your survey but with the minimal amount of pencil lead or ink and as quickly as possible. Closely related to the noncommitted respondent, a minimalist will not make full circles and will not fill in any of your open-ended questions, even if you have used sentence starters or provided the lines in which they could write. The minimalist has also been known to skip entire areas of the survey in his or her haste to get this task completed. All you can do is record the data as you see it; cell counts and computer programs will let you know if you have a big problem in this area. A second mailing will only result in their stealing the stamp and smiling on their way past the trash can as they pitch your precious survey.

The Extremist

These respondents can and will drive you crazy. They will go through your survey and rewrite your questions for you. They will not only answer every question, they will send you three additional pages of reference notes with full bibliographic information on your short answer or fill-in-the-blank questions. Extremists feel it is their professional obligation to complete your survey and also let you know every thought or concern or idea they ever had on your topic. The interesting thing with these types of returned surveys is that what they have usually scribbled in the margins, on the back of the pages, and within the context of your actual questions is often a repeat of a question you posed earlier. Seldom do their answers match their original thought when you asked the earlier question. All you can do at this point is open a file on your disk where you will record and analyze all other information. You will become a faster typist as a result of these respondents and will probably improve your scores next time you play Trivial Pursuit.

If you are now fully leaning toward the selection of another strategy, don't let the above stories scare you off. Consider it a challenge to do the best job possible in designing your survey or questionnaire and in identifying your population. The joys of manipulating data and producing descriptive and statistically significant findings are the number crunchers' nirvana. Just realize that for all those great surveys that you receive completed, you now have to analyze and figure out what those numbers may suggest or may seem to mean.

SECRETS CHECKLIST FOR INTERVIEWS

1. _____ Equipment:
   – Tape Recorder, tapes, and batteries
   – Portable microphone if extremely compulsive
   – Transcribing machine with tape size that matches other equipment
   – Paper, pens, paper clips, and a holder for this stuff, and consent forms
2. _____ List of questions
3. _____ Ideas to spark conversation if interviewee gives you the "Huh?" treatment
4. _____ Phone numbers for follow-up

SECRETS CHECKLIST FOR SURVEYS

1. _____ Good surveys can be basic and simple if you know what you're doing.

2. _____ Conduct pilot study.

3. _____ Make sure you have a survey type of population. If you don't think you will get an acceptable return rate, reread "A Tale of Two Methodologies" (Chapter 2) and punt.

4. _____ Check with an expert on the design of your survey or questionnaire.

5. _____ All items on your survey or questionnaire will have to be addressed in your writing.

Part II

The Secrets to Maintaining Sanity and Good Humor

6

Developing a Support Group

(aka Two Years Before the Last)

You most likely have formed some study groups during your tenure as a doctoral student. You can readily identify the colleagues who don't perform well in groups, who make inane comments in class that inspire you to roll your eyes in amazement, who miss more classes than they attend and then put you on the spot when they shamelessly beg to borrow your notes, and who always want to study with you but you are hard-pressed to even remember their full names. These are not the people you will choose for support at this critical time in your doctoral program. Frankly, you may not even want to share breathing space with these people anymore and certainly won't notify them of the time and date of your proposal defense.

After surviving the class work and embarking on the research and writing stage, you may begin to miss the student contacts after a while: Who else will you have to talk about, who will keep your life interesting? Who will you cheerfully advise to schedule his classes (opposite your schedule, of course) so you never have to hear his whiny voice again? Who will you learn to tune out while looking straight at her face? But now is not the time for wistful remembrances of jolly classroom tricks gone by. Now is the time to choose your real supporters (this is not to be confused with the selection of your committee members), those who will be there for you during this very lonely, very individual time. Now is also the time to know that by forming a solid support group, you are following Franklin's age-old advice: "We must all hang in there together, else we shall all hang separately."

For those of you who function well as a Lone Ranger and prefer to work entirely alone (or hang separately), you may choose to skip this chapter. However, many of you may decide to read this chapter twice.

Can You Fire-Walk Together?
(aka Wheels of Fire)

The best example we can give you is our personal story of how our group of three originally formed. We met at various times in early doctoral courses, saying little but watching everything. Two of us met at our first doctoral orientation and we bonded early as we had already identified students who fell in the categories previously mentioned. We volunteered for group projects together, and although we didn't take every course together, we all worked in some shape or form at the university we attended. (How else could we afford doctoral tuition?) For some reason, we knew we were a trio; we knew we shared many of life's truisms, yet we are as different as night and day. We discovered a similar irreverent sense of humor that probably drove others crazy as we shared subtle looks during classes. We often had a hard time not laughing, gloating, or yelling during serious discussions about adult development, Erikson, and feminist issues. We simply managed to bond and keep that bond tight, as anyone does in a valued friendship. We never wavered in our support of each other. We never complained about us, but we certainly complained about everything else and, frankly, we quickly gained a reputation for fire-walking with and for each other.

We were known for who we were individually but also because we associated with each other. Some faculty lamented the semesters when we all showed up for the same class; other faculty marveled at our support of each other. We were good students—we were probably some of the best. We knew how to play the game of academia and were willing to put in the required effort. We enjoyed our doctoral program in spite of all that you will read, but most of all we have enjoyed a friendship that we expect will last throughout our lifetimes. We still celebrate this relationship even though our programs have been successfully completed and we have regained a measure of sanity as we try to live normal postdoctorate lives. (We're not sure if writing a book is considered "normal," but we've enjoyed it immensely.)

These types of friendships continually grow and probably are one of those things you just have to accept as fate. It doesn't matter where you are in your program, and your group may be in different places, but when you find a few of these simpatico people, hang on to them. Enjoy those many, many nights you will see each other. Celebrate those classes that you can take together. Find out more about these potential supporters than simply asking if they finished the mountain of reading for the class you are about to attend. Find out about their lifestyles, their beliefs, their values, the real personalities outside the doctoral program. Go with these students to school events if you feel you must. Take the time to ask about their families, their spouses, their significant others, their children, and their pets. Take the time to mourn a frustrating grade and take the time to fly high when they accomplish a cherished goal or overcome a great fear. You have much responsibility as a group member and should you be as fortunate as we to find such solid friendships, realize that good relationships include compromise, give-and-take, tears, laughter, and many, many, many glasses of wine. (We shouldn't have to tell graduate students whom to go drinking with, but sometimes doctoral students become so immersed in course demands that they need a nudge to remember a much-needed personal life.)

Be Careful Whom You Choose
(aka Victims of Duty)

In your search for soul buddies, you may find yourself trying out groups that you regret 10 minutes after you make a heart-felt commitment. Don't be a victim. Try another one. This inner circle you choose has to pass some rigid requirements. They have to be able to choke back questions about your sudden weight gain. They have to be able to listen, listen, and listen to your dissertation lamentations time after time after time. They have to be able to see you through the bad hair days, the days when none of your apparel makes sense or your shoes don't match or you forgot your underwear. To be a member of a group this forgiving also implies reciprocity and you must follow the same rules. If you cannot listen, overlook, and laugh, you will not survive as a member.

This is not an easy process because it's difficult to predict who will tread lightly and safely with you, who will go down in flames, or who will simply slump down among the ashes and ignore everyone else. A word of caution: Beware of the needy folks who want to take large bites of your knowledge and energy, offering nothing in return. Sometimes called "emotional vampires," they are few in numbers but have powerful negative personalities. They can be difficult to detect, as they often first appear quite sweet and rational, but if you feel exhausted after 5 or 10 minutes with these vampires, or find communication to be a frustrating process, take the hint and run for cover. Remember, this is not the time to rehabilitate anyone. Put your Mother Theresa conscience to rest; this is not your job.

Beware also of the Darth Vaders who sabotage your work by giving you misleading information or offering only negative comments; the Tommy Talkers who seem able to babble without pausing for air and who quickly increase their volume to drown out your voice; High and Mighty Melvins who consider their opinions to be the only worthy ones; and the Fuzzy Freidas who offer long, divine discussions of the painfully obvious, numbing the entire class for the rest of the period. And there always are a few sweet-talkin', terminally cheerful Holy Henriettas who are so busy kissing up to the professor they forget to take notes and they constantly ask—fake smile securely glued in place—to borrow yours. None of these individuals should be considered for your support group.

Our group began with early traditions, rituals, and rules of operation. We quickly named ourselves AA (Attitude Adjustment) and we began scheduling regular meetings long before we began the dissertation process. We were well established before those dreaded qualifying exams. We were fair and honest with each other in sharing assignments, and spoke up honestly about what we felt we could or could not contribute. We traded tidbits about professors and respected each other's opinions but never hesitated to question something that felt off track. (Frankly, we don't disagree about too much, and even that usually creates a good laugh.) We never put one another on the spot, and rose to defend each other without hesitation. We relied heavily on honesty and humor. All these were unwritten rules, things we simply never questioned.

We also agreed not to invite a bunch of other members. We had several try to infiltrate, and after one dinner encounter of the worst kind, we made up an Attitude Adjustment Evaluation, practicing our newfound questionnaire skills, to see if future party crashers could pass our criteria. We didn't try to be elitists, but we felt we needed to be protective of our turf, our energy, and our relationship, and we knew from experience that large groups simply don't work. In our current postdoctoral euphoria, we are willing to share this top-secret evaluation with you for your future reference:

AA: ATTITUDE ADJUSTMENT EVALUATION

NAME OF GUEST: _____

	No	Somewhat	Yes
1. Did guest support any and all dissertation discussions, no matter how outrageous?	___	___	___
2. Did guest offer fair share of school gossip?	___	___	___
3. Did guest consume minimum required beverage (1 glass) and act increasingly silly?	___	___	___
4. Did guest offer sufficient relevant information on current students/staff/faculty?	___	___	___
5. Did guest willingly pay fair share of costs?	___	___	___
6. Did guest laugh readily, tell funny stories, and act completely unlike a doctoral student?	___	___	___
7. Did guest take a blood oath on confidentiality regarding the evening's conversation topics?	___	___	___
8. Did guest blatantly disregard all current forms of politically correct speech?	___	___	___
9. Will guest be invited back?	___	___	___
(Minimum requirements: 7 YES scores.) Total:	___	___	___

This is not to say that members of a support group cannot change or be flexible. In fact, as one of us finished the program, a second group formed with a different member, and it worked out well. Let's be honest: When you are facing the journey of a doctoral degree, with the intensity of the course work, the long, long hours you put in, and the massive amounts of money that you spend, the actual experience needs to be shared and lamented. No one else can understand, not the most loving and supportive spouse, not the most benevolent parents. No one else can argue the merits of the various methodologies with you. No one else can appreciate the immense change you have made in your life. A solid support group through the dissertation process will be the cherry Life Saver candy that time after time will not melt away as you savor the flavor.

The size of the group matters. We would suggest no more than three or four but recommend only three. This way you always have a 50/50 chance of making your point during those heavy philosophical discussions you will have over the choice of committee members or the upcoming exam or the latest rumor or gossip you have heard. Larger groups don't work. Too many people means too much talking, too many splinter groups, too many opinions to sift through, too many clashing personalities. We have all had frustrating experiences with groups that disintegrate into bedlam; you know what we're talking about. Keep the size to three or four and give yourselves a name such as the Three (Four) Musketeers, the Three (Four) Stooges, the Triumphant Trio, the Quadratic Equation, or the Good, the Bad, and the Ugly (well, maybe not that one).

We've assembled a checklist of qualities that one must have to be considered for the high honor of your support group membership. (True to our doctoral training, we make endless lists then make lists of lists.) This list applies to all times, not just dinner meetings. We named this one too.

TOP TEN TERMS OF ENDEARMENT

_____ 1. Will members willingly lift your spirits when the committee turns down your best proposal ideas?

_____ 2. Will members continue to lament your less-than-perfect grade for weeks, maybe even months, even if they are desperately longing for new subjects for lamentations?

_____ 3. Will members call you, bug you, force you away from the computer even though you have refused to take their calls?

_____ 4. Will members only snicker, but not laugh out loud, when you confess you carry working drafts of your dissertation in your car and have stashed one set in a file cabinet at work and another with a friend?

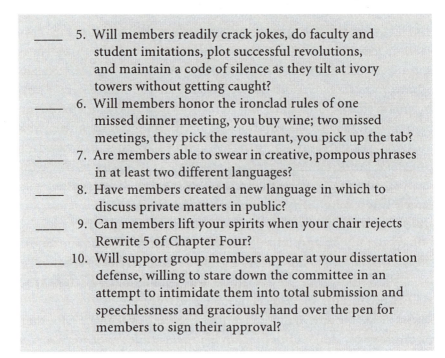

_____ 5. Will members readily crack jokes, do faculty and student imitations, plot successful revolutions, and maintain a code of silence as they tilt at ivory towers without getting caught?

_____ 6. Will members honor the ironclad rules of one missed dinner meeting, you buy wine; two missed meetings, they pick the restaurant, you pick up the tab?

_____ 7. Are members able to swear in creative, pompous phrases in at least two different languages?

_____ 8. Have members created a new language in which to discuss private matters in public?

_____ 9. Can members lift your spirits when your chair rejects Rewrite 5 of Chapter Four?

_____ 10. Will support group members appear at your dissertation defense, willing to stare down the committee in an attempt to intimidate them into total submission and speechlessness and graciously hand over the pen for members to sign their approval?

If you can answer yes to all of the above questions (no wiggle room allowed in this list), then you have finally found those few people who will indeed fire-walk with you. Guard them with your heart; they will be there for you at your worst and at your best. They will just be there, always.

Early in the development of our group, we forced ourselves to set up monthly dinner meetings. We would allow flexibility because of school schedules, family commitments, and holidays, but we would never go past six weeks without a gathering. Because humans have a tendency to reprioritize their lives in that amount of time, we set up a rule that if a person cancels a meeting, they have to pay the bill the next time out. (In more than four years, only one person has had to pick up the dinner tab.) This is the only way to keep a support group going. Force a scheduled time and always, always, meet it. It can be as simple as the second Tuesday of each month or as elaborate as the first Saturday after the first Sunday on even days when the sun doesn't shine, but set the standard early. It quickly becomes a beacon of hope and sanity on both good days and those days when your self-doubt is raging out of control.

A neutral area in which to meet, away from the usual university environment (and those ever-present eavesdroppers) is best. Sharing of food and refreshment seems to soothe frustrations and add ambiance to each meeting. It's been easiest for us to meet during the week; you may find other times work better. The time schedule is also flexible, and we found that our meetings usually ran for about 2 to $2\frac{1}{2}$ hours. Breakfasts, lunches, dinners, whatever works for your group—just do it.

Sometimes we have specific agendas and sometimes we don't. Sometimes we solve about 50 little problems; sometimes we're in the mood to blow off everything serious and just eat and laugh and pretend to have real lives. We are scattered all over the county, so we change locations frequently. All you really want is an easy-to-reach place that is fun, serves good food, and will let you hang out at the table long after the check has been paid. You don't want to feel this is a pressing meeting but a gathering in interest of your mental health. It's like a therapy session with hang-loose therapists who really care for you. It's a safe time to relax and enjoy the company as well as get all those frustrations with your writing, your committee, your topic, your analysis, and your life out in the open.

One final word of advice: Don't wait until near the end of your program to work on the formation of a support group. Try not to let the opportunity for good times and great laughs pass you by until you get to the dissertation phase. If you are lucky like we were, you'll hit the right combination the first time, but if not, don't worry, there are good companions out there and they need you as much as you need them.

Loneliness Happens (aka I Wonder as I Wander)

In spite of a terrific support group and loyal family members and pets, when you get right down to the writing process, you have to do it alone. No one can do it for you, and many times students feel abandoned. Dissertation writing is a lonely process, and you might as well get that into your head early so the shock won't be too discouraging. It is certainly true that some students actually revel in this alone time, cheerfully shutting their doors and turning telephones off so they can wallow in their wonderful words for weeks at a time. These students don't need this section: Go back to your cave and have a great time. The rest of you might keep reading.

Our research tells us that this seems to be a particularly difficult time for women, especially for those who gain strength and energy from relationships and who have not experienced a great deal of encouragement or support in their academic progression. It has been well documented that many women struggle with the male-dominated methods and mind-set of academic discourse in which an atmosphere of challenge and criticism dominates the academic process.

This is a tender gender issue, because it has been well documented that males tend to dominate classroom discussion and activities from grade school through graduate-level programs. Boys often receive the most attention, are rewarded for speaking out of turn or being loud, and receive the most positive feedback for exploring creative solutions. Girls, on the other hand, tend to be rewarded for being "good," being silent and acquiescent, and often receive negative feedback for high energy, mental enthusiasm, or a willingness to argue an academic point. Although recognition of these classroom biases is increasing, we are often told by teachers at all levels that old habits die hard, and the general classroom atmosphere, from grade school to graduate school, still favors the male animal. That knowledge may chase some women out of school, but many others are inspired to stand firm and fight the degree-conferring dragons, which we encourage mightily.

But whatever your gender and previous experience, if you have made it to this level you are clearly a successful student, so pat yourself on the back and let's get on with another area of challenge—our skittery emotional states.

Dealing With Emotions (aka Voices of Silence)

For those of you who feel truly lonely, and it's OK to admit it, we have a few suggestions. First, recognize this is a solitary phase and simply make the best of it. Use those positive thinking skills and tell yourself this is your most exciting and rewarding time, what you've worked for all these years, even if your mind keeps snapping at you in the middle of your affirmations, "Yeah, right, what a joke." Second, if your committee members are interested in your topic, responsive to your questions, and willing to offer you time as mentor/adviser, you will actually enjoy this stage. We encountered many professors who thoroughly enjoy this process of guiding students over the final hurdles and beam with pride when the ideas and organization and chapters come together seamlessly. We also have heard of a few who would just as soon encourage you to leave school and never return. Choose wisely.

Moby's Sick . . .

. . . and tired of the whole thing. And we don't blame you because this is one of the emotions that seems to play out the most, in both men and women, of all ages, and in many programs. You've struggled through many difficult classes, spent countless hours on frivolous and side issues, and jumped through many rigorous academic hoops that have been carefully preserved since Aristotle was a toddler. Frankly, emotionally you may feel as dry as the desert.

It's easy to get sick and tired of the process, and this may be the real reason for the 50% dropout rate, not the lack of classes with regular student contact, not unavailable professors or a wobbly support group, but an overwhelming feeling of being sick and tired of the entire challenge. You tremble at the thought of having to ask another question, transcribe another interview, search out another potential theme, triangulate any more data, run more stats, or analyze additional post hoc findings.

But in spite of being sick and tired of the whole thing, you still, if you ever want to wear that hot, heavy cap and gown, have to finish the research and write it up. We have no simple or secret shortcuts to overcome being sick and tired, except to gather strength from your support group and then go back home and continue to slog through each chapter to give yourself just enough incentive to lurch on to the next one.

Just when exhaustion is chomping on your soul, someone (yes, it will be a committee member) will suggest you "do a complete rewrite of Chapter Four," which is already 179 pages long and simply cannot be rewritten within a normal life span. Sometimes simply saying the word "no" is enough to stimulate a compromise, if you can adequately—and passionately—defend your position. (Falling in a dead faint on the book-strewn office carpet has been known to work, too.) Either action may startle the committee members so much they may rethink the request and an alternative plan can be worked out. Or else, guess what? You go home and rewrite it.

> *TOP SECRET:* This is when you hire a professional editor and tell your committee exactly what you are doing. Once the committee knows you have brought in a hired gun, they most often will leave you alone. They are probably grateful to have it out of their hands. But you *do* have to do exactly what the editor advises.

Dorian Is Getting Gray

And so are you, all your friends, and certainly your parents, as well as the staff at the university and anyone else over 28. This is a process that encourages gray hairs to sprout as quickly as dandelions after a rainstorm. Did you really expect otherwise?

It's a cliché that no one is getting any younger. It's an axiom that people in doctoral programs age faster than those living normal lives. No statistics here, just take our word for it. There's nothing you can do except whiz through as fast as you can, remember to take long walks, sneak off to good restaurants, and keep bottles of Excedrin in every room and book bag. Your support group will party hearty with you for many years to come, for they are the ones who truly understand where you have been.

SECRETS CHECKLIST

1. _____ Find a group who will take you.

2. _____ Set up nonnegotiable ground rules.

3. _____ Keep the panic in perspective; it's only temporary.

4. _____ Rely on your support group and whatever other activity keeps you going. (We leave some things up to your imagination and personal lifestyle.)

5. _____ Keep your sense of humor—it's the best weapon in your arsenal.

<h1 align="center">7</h1>

Getting Organized

(aka Hidden Habits of
Demented Dissertation Writers)

Any habit, whether hidden or not, will cause slipping and sliding if you go against your normal modes of operation. After all, you have had at least 16 years of academic practice to perfect your neurotic habits, and we all have them. That's why this chapter is addressing an assortment of topics that may create serious slippage if ignored, topics that may seem small by themselves but are important to the overall process. Remember the old adage from Eldridge Cleaver, "You are either part of the solution or part of the problem."

Most people who have reached this stage are clearly intelligent (although this process will be a real test of that conclusion) and competent in various higher thinking skills that will be put to great use in completing the dissertation. Of course you will work hard, but you are now so close that you also need to work smart. Face it, you have given up several years of your life to complete courses that are usually held late at night, missed dinners several times a week, skidded through more books than you even realized were published, written more papers about topics you suspect were of extraterrestrial origins, suffered through enough exams to further test your stamina in redundancy, and may have even done something called qualifying exams. You have earned—and you certainly deserve—the right to pay yet more money (up to 10 units more of course work) for this time academia cheerfully refers to as "The Dissertation." If you are paying for it, then get your money's worth.

One habit worth cultivating is that of an obsessive-compulsive saver of thoughts, ideas, quotes, concepts, and miscellaneous brainstorms for your dissertation. Put them on a disk if you wish, labeling them by such names as leadership, change, paradigms, references, working titles, power, voices, lives, organizations, methodology requirements, or whatever topics pertain to your own work. Make sure those obsessive buttons also push you to record the bibliographic information and page numbers—critical information if you decide you need this. As the disk fills, you will know that progress toward your dissertation is indeed being made, and now you have flexible lists.

Another nifty habit is to fine-tune your research by investigating your school, college, or department dissertation library. (We assume you have access to the hard work of those who have gone before and survived.) Flip through these neatly bound books, getting a feel for structure, organization, format, methodology, style, and key words or phrases that keep popping up like a hyperactive circus clown. This research may be especially helpful when developing your methodological defense strategies, often a sticky point for beginning researchers.

Please don't expect a template for your dissertation, however. Such a creature does not exist, and it shouldn't. You would only be filling in blanks, not conducting original research with original style and your individual discussion of your particular results.

Also, don't be surprised if you find tiny typos, quirky commas, or funky phrases that seem out of place. No dissertation is error-free, and because you probably didn't attend that particular proposal defense, you are not privy to midstream changes.

But you can jump-start your brain by listening to ongoing proposal defenses, if you are allowed to sit in on them. Most are open, but you may have to continually check with professors, colleagues, or the secretary to learn when they are scheduled. Some people try to avoid audiences by scheduling their defenses early in the morning or during working hours, or simply don't want anyone except the committee in attendance. That is a policy you will have to discover.

A good technique for researching committee members is to attend dissertation defenses; the information you gain about committee members and potential chairs will be invaluable when you begin that process. (These events may be somewhat intimidating, but you will be at this stage soon, and your elation will carry the day.) If the topic is even remotely related to yours, think of what you can learn by talking with that person. A brand-new doctor is only too happy to share the journey she or he has just completed. Don't be dismayed if they are reluctant to hand you full copies of their bibliographies, however; these lists are still a work in progress until the ink has dried on the final approval forms.

When Everything Is in Pieces (aka Humpty Dumpty)

Facing the actual dissertation writing can be nerve-wracking. Beware the "I'll Never Get It Done" Syndrome, which tends to pop out like hives at various stages of preparation. You may have defended a proposal, cleared human subjects, and be well launched in your actual research. Now you join the lonely hearts club band. There are no scheduled classes to attend; there is no professor outlining your life day by day, week by week. You may have lost your only network of people that actually care if you ever graduate, your peers. Now is the time for perseverance, commitment to your goals, and discipline. Put the pieces back together again, not your life but your dissertation pieces.

Whatever you do, don't try to change your style or work habits now. You will only get more frustrated and feel more depressed that you can't accomplish anything while trying to change. It will be like trying to feed the multitudes, biblically speaking, with one loaf of bread and three fish. With your boxes, files, computer disks, and backpacks full of papers, it's now time to put them all together in some form or format that works for you. Starting by sorting the piles around the perimeter of your work room is known to help, but be careful to label each pile with a stickie on the wall and don't vacuum or allow frisky four-legged creatures into this area.

One method of overcoming writer's block is to take your proposal and rewrite it in the past tense. After all, you have now completed your research and your actual dissertation will be in the past tense. While you are at this task, you can finally begin fitting all those important subsections into your final version of the first three chapters. The headings for these chapters do not change, and given that you have been there and done that, it is a nice way to start. It can give you great confidence to tell people that you are working on Chapter One, Two, or even Three. There are usually only five chapters in total, although some people do have six. Also, don't despair if everything you have already collected doesn't fit; this is typical and can be the basis for your ongoing study or work, postdissertation.

At this point, it is also a wise strategy to update your bibliography. Whether you are using *APA*, *Chicago*, Campbell's, or Turabian (not to be confused with the family of fast-galloping horses), you will need to be accurate and you certainly don't want to be searching for an elusive page number or wandering volume number as you approach D day. Remember, it is easier to delete something than to retrieve it.

There are a few life-savers we have included in the Emergency Appendectomy section that you may find useful: ways to introduce quotes (Appendix A), a comprehensive checklist that gives you more specifics internally by chapter section (Appendix B), a statistical decision tree to help you decide on the correct statistical treatment to use (Appendix C), and a list of verbs to spark your writing in Appendix D. These materials can guide you in fitting each puzzle piece into a finished product.

If you are doing a quantitative study, run your data and data tables, construct your tables in a file that will allow you to insert them into your text as you are writing, and remember when you are doing this kind of work that you are actually working on Chapter Four. If you are doing a qualitative study, construct your demographic table or outline of your participant(s). You know who your participants are.

If you are still stymied, try writing your abstract. It is something that can be done in less than 500 words and you can see an end to this one step. If that is too far down the road, try writing your "pre-pages." The acknowledgment or dedication page is always a fun thing to do and gives you an opportunity to count your blessings as you are still struggling with the actual writing. Set up your table of contents, even if all you have are the headings from your proposal. This is quite satisfying and convinces your brain that you are actually working on your dissertation. You can even start Chapter Five, as the first pages are simply a restatement of your earlier chapters in the summary section. Sometimes the more mundane tasks can be easily accomplished and you will find the diversion from thinking about your data refreshing. Also, there is the remote possibility that you will have a brainstorm in what your collected data are saying to you and you can always go back to it. That's the beauty of computers and individual files.

All the pieces will finally come together but you can't force the issue and you can't wait until the last moment. You may want to consider setting an appointment with yourself. Pencil your name in your daily book for a specific amount of time and keep your appointment. Some days you may just sit at the computer, drumming your fingers on the keyboard, feeling the time is wasted. Other days you may get so invigorated that the time goes by and your flying fingers will hate to stop. Be prepared, there will be plenty of both of these. But at least you have made the effort and you will find out in the long run whether making an appointment with yourself works for you. Only you will discover—or already know—if you work best in short sprints or marathon distance endeavors.

Getting Control of Your Life (aka Time Marches On)

Many say that the next great age that will be historically noted is the Time Age. We have romped through the Stone Age, the Agricultural Age, the Industrial Age, the Information Age, the Postindustrial Age, and the who-knows-what age, but the experts (who are they, anyway?) predict that the only thing left to conquer is the issue of time. Many have tried to give us management tips for time, and we all know them well. We also realize that they only work to a certain extent because real life often steps in and brings us crashing back to the reality that time is only a type of measuring what we haven't completed, what we forgot to do yesterday, what appointment we missed, or that our favorite watch needs a new battery. Time management tips often make one feel that one doesn't manage time well and so defeat their purpose. Of course, these issues of time don't have anything to do with PST, Daylight Savings, or EST, except when trying to get the best long-distance rates, but they do apply to real issues of organization and strategies that will work the best for you.

As with many secrets in this book, we will give you an amended version of time management tips. Some are tried, true, and tested; others make good common sense; and a couple sound like they might work if we had the energy to try them. It is at this point that some self-evaluation of your real strengths and weaknesses will be valuable. An honest evaluation of your concepts of time management will help you beat the odds and actually complete the dissertation.

The following are some time management ideas that may appeal to your own sense of structure.

The Mad Hatter: I'm Late, I'm Late, I'm Very Very Late

Perhaps you will need to consider two sets of deadlines for every major step of your process to convince your brain that although you will always be late, you won't be too late. Give yourself a break and keep to your original time line or deadline, even though you are one of those optimistic folks who keeps setting impossible deadlines. If you have a second deadline that is more realistic, you may find that you aren't that late after all. Having one of your buddies remind you that you are going to be late, whether it is a poke in the ribs or a kick in the pants, may just be the encouragement you need to meet the deadline with your sanity intact. Watch out for getting ahead of your deadlines, however; someone will simply encourage you to make more revisions of that terminally long Chapter Four—and who would wish that on themselves?

Scarlet Lives On and On and On

Are you the type who thinks tomorrow is actually just another day? If so, you need to wake up: Tomorrow will truly arrive in just a few short hours, and there is no way you can postpone the inevitable. You may need a perpetual calendar or maybe one of those newfangled alarms that keeps beeping until tomorrow is actually here, reminding you that you'd better get cracking. If you have a snippet of competition lurking inside your tired body, set up a schedule with one of your support group and have a contest to keep each other going. Report in when you have completed Chapter One or when your list of literature sources reaches a desired number. Check in when you have completed the first interview or conducted your first treatment. Celebrate for a day by taking in a movie or having dinner with friends, then go back to work.

High Noon at the O.K. Corral:
Shoot Your Way Out

Some people with high self-esteem and a crooked sense of timing may rely on their ability to verbally shoot their way out of a problem. These are the ones who don't bother to rehearse a speech, who figure one afternoon in the library blowing dust out of book bindings is enough, who will march into a dissertation defense and simply shoot out anything that pops into their heads. This is Time Management at its loosest, a form of Russian roulette that isn't recommended for anyone on a doctoral journey. But sometimes the right person, standing in the right corral, will blaze both guns, blow away the smoke, and walk away victorious. We're incredibly jealous of that talent and wish we had cultivated it long ago.

Transylvania Time: Are You a Night Person?

Some folks are night wanderers, insisting they have their best ideas when the houses and streets are quiet, when the telephone is turned off, and when their roommates or families are snoring peacefully in another room. Their adventures are silent but effective, and their results aren't nearly as messy or gory as we might think. In fact, some of their writings turn out to be spectacularly successful. If you long for shorter days and longer nights, you just might be a night wanderer, so face up to it and plan accordingly. No sense in resetting your entire biological clock just for a few chapters; just go with your biorhythms and enjoy the quiet times.

No, No, a Thousand Times No

Are you able to say no to favors, fun times, fund-raising chair positions, family reunions, and frolicking in the park on Sunday afternoons? Because if you are ever going to gain control over your days and nights, and manage your time efficiently, the first lesson to learn is to say no. Say it regretfully, say it remorsefully, say it with clenched teeth, or say it with joy—but say it loud and clear. The world is full of Time Zappers who will steal your time if you allow them, so put all your good deeds on hold and use the word *no* freely. You'll be glad you did.

Qualitative Coding (aka Ten Little, Nine Little, Eight Little Stickies)

A particularly effective strategy for wading through the pages and pages of qualitative interview data is to pick a good organization strategy. During the collection process, you won't think too much about how you are going to organize all this. The problem smacks you in the face when you stumble over one powerful sentence while thumbing through notebooks. If you did not transcribe your own data, you may want to listen to your tapes again to pick up voice inflection, nuances, or specific language that may be critical to your interpretation of the results.

When faced with this voluminous amount of real, rich, and deep data, your brain will actually question your sanity in taking on this task in the first place. Qualitative data will and often does seem insurmountable, but you have to move beyond these feelings into the world of reality: coding. Even using brightly colored high-light pens won't resolve the coding problems because you will still be thumbing through pages of materials and trying to pull similar thoughts into some kind of coherent pattern or theme. One of us tried a system of tape flags, which worked well. Assuming you have determined your overall themes, give each theme a color code and match them to those great inventions called tape flags. These are stickie notes that can be stuck on the edge of the page and protrude enough for you to see the color. They are easily removable and won't harm or erase or smudge your actual text. They come in about seven to ten different colors and are fairly inexpensive to purchase at those mammoth office supply stores.

You will need to reread your transcripts, placing the color-coded stickies directly on the page where that theme seems to jump out for you. When you finish, you will have a rainbow of protrusions from your text. You may even have more than one in the same spot, but at least you have a start at organizing your qualitative data.

From there, it is up to you how you pull it all together. We color-coded the themes, then collected the various parts of the sentences, words, or quotes for that theme (be careful that in retyping these you identify the speaker) into one file (again, assuming you are making use of your computer's capability). When you finish with one color, go directly to another color and start another new file. Continue with this until you have identified all your salient data for each theme or pattern. You can then print out each theme and write from those notes, with the references to the speaker and their actual words right at hand. You can even go as far as printing the themes on the corresponding color of paper that matches your tabs. If you are an anal-retentive type, self-diagnosed and proud of it, of course, find the smaller tape flags (five colors to a package). Use these for subthemes and place them directly on larger tape flags. The goal is to make a vivid rainbow. If you fail to see many colors, go back and start again. But in any case, you can then put your transcripts aside and work from your superorganized system of themes.

A word of warning: Don't be concerned with the amount of data you collected that you don't use; this is very common and also a good sign that you have done true qualitative research. There will be much to be discarded and much to be set aside. It's just like in quantitative research when you have insignificant findings but you still have to run the statistical treatments; finding the few gems of significance amounts to finding gold in them thar hills. The same is true for qualitative research, as you probably found throughout your interviews and observations.

Statistics (aka In the Labyrinth)

Probably the biggest mistake that doctoral candidates make in choosing their analysis strategy is to automatically dismiss any statistical procedure if they have the choice of either a quantitative or a qualitative methodology. We've heard the wails in the hallways, "But I'm math-o-phobic, I can't juggle all those numbers!" Might as well get over it right now, because some of you will not have a choice, depending upon the discipline you are in and the ontological and epistemological preferences and beliefs of your department/school/college. Too many of us vividly remember the hours of staring at statistics books in our courses, the many hours of burst spreadsheets that made absolutely no sense, and actually wondering why post hoc tests were even invented, much less why we had to actually understand the coefficient of the mean and the estimated error variance of that mean. So, realizing that the land of qualitative (as in "no statistics") studies existed was like a joyous bolt from the heavens.

If there are any secrets to working with statistical data, they are more in the actual presentation of the data and the statistical program you are working with. (If you have chosen to hire a professional number cruncher for this odious task, then you only have to make sure you understand all the analysis so that you can competently write about it as well as competently defend your findings.) The secret here is to be as familiar with the analysis program as you can. It is quite simple: You will become quite intimate with your numbers, findings, tables, levels of significance, and the very real possibility of having to develop secondary hypotheses and analyze interaction effects.

There are some fairly basic computer statistical programs on the market that can make this process easier and that are designed with the struggling student in mind. Two of the most used are STATVIEW SE and STATVIEW SE + GRAPHICS (for Macs) and MYSTAT (for both MACS and IBM/PC), although EXCEL programs are now being used more frequently. These programs are user-friendly, have a very thorough user's guide, and even offer explanations of what your data findings may mean. They are relatively inexpensive but do require a fairly thorough understanding of the statistical procedure of choice. There are also mainframe programs such as SPSS available for personal computers. However, many universities have this program and will let students use it for free. It may be the only portion of this process that is free, so you might as well explore the options.

The real secret to success is to adhere to the required format for presentation of your data. In some cases, you will have to fully retype your findings into a table format. In other cases, you can cut and paste your significant tables directly into your text, a task made easier if you find out beforehand how this works with your program of choice. In addition, it is very important to realize that your data findings, in most programs we have worked with, cannot be saved, except possibly as text. So, once you have done your analysis (performed your *t*-test, ANOVA, or correlation and deleted outliers that skew your data), print it out, then you have all the necessary information that you will need as you are writing up your findings.

Also, be aware that many of these statistical programs have wondrous tools that allow you to change the size of your graphics, headers, and footers, and also allow you to manipulate the presentation of the data, especially in the case of bar graphs. Again, remember that once you have spent countless hours inserting that bar graph title, print it out to be sure it is what you want, because you may have to start from scratch if you can't save that particular significant finding.

Statistical analysis is only clean if you have entered the data correctly in the right categories, combined or collapsed the categories, and chosen the correct statistical treatment for your data and resolution of your hypotheses. In the Emergency Appendectomy section you will find a decision tree that may help you make critical choices.

Before you begin your data entry, or shortly after you begin, print out portions of your database, paste them on the wall, and look for missing cells or for numbers like 45 if you did a survey with only 1 through 5 choices on a Likert scale. Yes, it takes time, but it's necessary if you want to have findings that are meaningful. A number like 45 in a cell can really create havoc with your mean scores. Take a sample of your database to your local statistical guru or mentor or committee member and talk through your process of data entry. You will be glad to have someone else to talk with about these numbers but, better than that, you can rest a bit more easily knowing that your database is theoretically correct. A significant hint here is that if you choose to skip this step and all your findings turn out to be either highly significant ($p < .0000001$) or none of your findings appears to be significant, then you most likely have entered your data incorrectly or have chosen the wrong statistical treatment. Building a good database is like building a good sand castle; it cannot be constructed on quicksand or wrecked by a rogue wave.

A final thought on the preparation of your data findings is that the presentation of findings is a critical piece in the acceptance of your results. In most cases, varying the presentation, except in the case of statistical analyses tables, is greatly appreciated by the reader of your chapter. Don't be afraid to present demographic baseline data in pie charts, to present categorical variables like age, occupation, and years of experience using frequency distributions, and simple yes-no answers or responses in visual graphic form. There is something quite satisfying to the reader in seeing the balance or lack of balance in a dramatic visual presentation rather than reading about it (although every table, chart, or figure is written about as if it were not right there in the middle of the page for all the world to see); it makes a greater impact on what you are purporting to have found through your research.

Hoops and Troughs (aka Over the River and Through the Woods)

As with any bureaucratic process, institutions of higher learning adhere to process and procedure as one of their final "got-ya's." The dissertation procedure has hoops and barrels you must work through to complete the process. There are usually forms that have to be filed, time lines that have to be met, procedures that have to be followed—and the list goes on. A quick guideline to most of this process is usually found in a doctoral handbook that is published by the departments, colleges, or schools that you are attending. We were given a one-inch binder of instructions, forms, formats, and procedures that were our responsibility to follow. The last chapter outlined, quite completely, our responsibilities in the dissertation process. This information should be committed to memory as you don't want your big day to come and find out that you haven't prepared your announcement correctly or that your chair has not reserved the room for your defense. Don't take any of these procedures lightly. As the old Boy Scout motto says, "Be prepared."

Local-level rules, regulations, and procedures supersede those of nationally published guidelines such as *APA*. Written policies such as notification of faculty and students of your defense dates, petitions for advancement to candidacy, petitions to graduate, and formatting instructions, as well as copies that are necessary, must all be adhered to in the end, and you should be on top of these from the starting gun. Don't assume that someone will notify you when these are due; take the responsibility to meet the deadlines. Remember, nothing as mundane as a form not being filed should deter you at this point. You have enough on your mind in creating and writing your wonderful contribution to the field or discipline. If your individual department or school does not have this information, contact your graduate division and find out all that you can; you'll be grateful that you have tied up all those loose ends.

Now, to the bad news: There is documented research that the dissertation process is more like a wave (somebody probably did this as a doctoral dissertation, what a topic!) (see Figure 7.1). As your eyes slide down the dissertation wave, don't get discouraged. David Sternberg believes in an optimistic view, that each successive stage is generally easier because of your prior successes. Expect periods of high frustration, high anxiety, self-doubt, and desperation as well as periods of elation, creativity, and high levels of satisfaction. The best advice in the down periods of time is to realize that these feelings are normal. You should talk it out with a trusted, fellow doctoral student or your support group buddies. Sharing helps bring the bad times into a more balanced perspective. You can also give yourself a break, take some time, even plan on a change of scenery. Renew family relationships, don't touch the computer, take walks, and have a real life. This is important to your sanity and often will come in the middle of a writing period or slump. Your overall planning and time lines should allow for this break.

One of us became so upset over an unexpected grade in a course that she lost six weeks of research time during her study. She finally talked it out with her chair, who reminded her that grades are irrelevant at this point and to let it go; what was important was that she not let the SOB (silly old boy, of course) affect the ultimate goal of completing her degree. It was a lose-lose situation for the

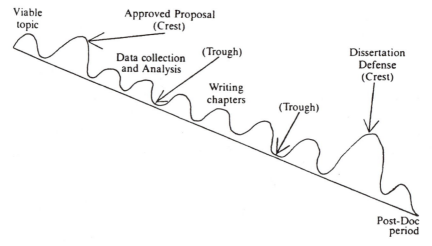

Figure 7.1. The Dissertation Wave
SOURCE: Copyright © 1981 by David Sternberg, from *How to Complete and Survive a Doctoral Dissertation*, by David Sternberg. Reprinted by permission of St. Martin's Press Incorporated.

student and was in some ways reinforcing the professor's opinion that her work was not important. She had the last laugh, however: Her dissertation won international recognition and she was given the Outstanding Doctoral Student award at the commencement ceremonies. Sometimes there is divine justice in the world.

As a writer you will sometimes be down in the dumps or troughs, or wallowing in one or more of the "three Ds"—known as the dissertation Depression, Doubt, or Desperation Syndrome—and sometimes you will ride the crests of relative elation or satisfaction with your research. Knowing what to expect often helps you get through both the hoops and the troughs, and steers you back to your more important work, completing the dissertation.

How to Avoid the Withering Frights

As with hoops and troughs, there will be periods of downright scary times. You will start to doubt yourself, your ability, your overachieving attitude, and your confidence. These can come at unexpected times and be caused by unexpected events. Even the best-laid plans of mice and men go astray. A period to be aware of involves the "Do I Have Enough Literature Review?" or the "I Can't Find Anything in the Literature on My Topic" Syndrome. When this disease attacks, take two aspirin, go for a long walk, then reassess your literature review strategies. If you are now trying to find the holy grail, you have gone too far in your search. If you are seeing repetitions of the same names as you do more reading, you have probably reached saturation. If you are staring at more than one box full of photocopied references, then it is time to quit. You probably have enough literature to write three dissertations. If, on the other hand, you have yet to find something, you are probably not using the right descriptors to access your information.

In a dissertation about meeting the needs of *graduate students through nontraditional programs,* each word of the topic was used as a descriptor to access through ERIC and other sources of appropriate literature. The only source that was eventually found after hours on the computer and in the dungeons of the library was a study on the choice of a graduate program from 1936. Its relevancy was sure to be questioned by the committee of the doctoral student at the proposal defense.

On one of our frequent (and sometimes frustrating) visits to the university library, we discovered a flyer announcing that doctoral students could meet with a librarian to assist in identifying resources. As a last resort, we approached the library research assistant. This creative young lady, after hearing the details of the dissertation, calmly remarked, "Well, it seems to me that you should try the descriptor *marketing of graduate programs.*" When we punched in the word *marketing,* a number of more recent studies surfaced through Brigham Young University. Obviously this provided a wealth of information and additional resources that were perfect for the literature review. So, the moral is to use even the most remote of sources. If you don't find anything, you're probably not looking in the right places.

Fear in all forms may cause anxiety and high blood pressure, but a certain amount of creative tension adds to the adrenaline flow and puts one in top shape and form. Don't let fear drive you to the point that you are not operational. A proposal defense for one student was set for a morning conference. The prospective candidate followed the usual routine of preparing the defense the night before; she had slept well, had the appropriate apparel identified, and was ready to go two hours before the 9:00 a.m. time. With nothing to do except get more anxious, the candidate drove to the university and sat in her car for those two hours. As the time was nearing to go to the designated room, the candidate felt momentarily paralyzed. Fear had overtaken every plan, every ounce of confidence, and every other bodily function. Fear of failing, fear of the unknown, just plain fear of not making the grade.

Thankfully, one of the committee members noticed the unmoving candidate and came over to wish her success at the defense. The committee member recognized the anxiety attack symptoms and took drastic measures by opening the car door and saying the very reassuring words, "Well, I haven't quite finished reading the proposal yet." That put everything into proper perspective. This scenario can happen to anyone, but a healthy dose of courage and determination will drive out the fear and propel you to your next step.

Another doctoral candidate was preparing her overheads for her final doctoral defense. Candidates are limited to an approximately 20-minute presentation (in which time it is hard to summarize the 400-some pages that you have recently given birth to). Time limits are strictly adhered to; after all, doctoral faculty are very busy people with tight schedules to keep. When the candidate was called by one of her buddy team to wish her success, she commented that she was ready, she had over 24 overheads prepared for her presentation. She was reminded that she only had 20 minutes and that was more than 1 per minute. Her comment was, "I guess I didn't think about that, I really am ready, aren't I?"

You may never be fear-free until after all is said and done, but you can be on the alert for any signs leading to a panic attack. Have support available. If you have submitted your best work, completed your homework with your committee, planned and organized your presentations, rehearsed your presentations, and generally pulled yourself together to be ready and primed for action, there is no one person or environment or set of events that can override what you know. You have spent countless hours of time in conducting research, and you are now confident of your own findings. You have followed procedures and met all the rules and regulations. You are now the expert on your particular topic. The very worst that can happen is that you will have to do some rewriting, probably in Chapter Five, "Summary, Conclusions, and Recommendations." This is very common and should not be seen as a judgment of your worth. Chapter Five was your final chance to say what you think, what you found, what you believe, and what you are. Of course, there will be disagreement; some committees feel it is their obligation to literally have a defense (in the combative sense) but you will persevere and you will ultimately reach your goal.

SECRETS CHECKLIST

1. _____ Do whatever it takes to get started.
2. _____ Remain true to your style of writing and work habits.
3. _____ Rewrite your proposal in the past tense.
4. _____ Take a break when times get rough.
5. _____ Construct your data tables or participant outlines.
6. _____ In data analysis, try strategies such as flag notes or variations of presenting numerical findings.
7. _____ Write your abstract.
8. _____ Work on your "pre-pages."

8

Using Technology

(aka Gone With the Windows)

The end of the twentieth century has seen advances that many of us never imagined to be possible. Some of us can too readily remember using a simple typewriter to prepare papers for undergraduate course work. Imagine having to retype entire pages or use a bottle of "white out" to hide errors—not to mention the hand drawing of charts and graphs!

For the dissertation writer, the computer becomes a third appendage for the duration of the process. Be prepared, however, to have a love-hate relationship with this machine and a full complement of peripherals that you think you will need but may not know how to use. Be prepared also to realize that Murphy's Law applies in this world as well, and "What can go wrong, will go wrong." You may not be in the "computer geek" category, scanning through computer magazines like Data Dweeb, making comments like, "Whoa, check out the 6X SCSI-2 CD-ROM on *that* baby!" but it helps to know someone who is.

Learning the Language
(aka The Fear Slayer)

Technology is the great equalizer among us all. It certainly proves that illiteracy is alive and well on the information highway. Just ask any young child how to retrieve e-mail or get on the Internet and her modem-speed mind will spit out words like *folders, files, attachments, URLs, web sites, home pages,* and addresses that have more dots than 101 Dalmatians. But you also need to become familiar with new words and instant resources. Where else can you find that final reference you so desperately need to complete your bibliography at 3 a.m. on a Sunday morning even if you have to access a library in Timbuktu? We know one doctoral student who put his name on a listserv regarding charter schools. Within two weeks he received enough material to fill a two-inch binder full of demographic information and references to charter schools throughout the United States from the Director of the Office of Education in Washington, D.C.

The computer world has a language of its own, and to say that you should strongly consider becoming bilingual is an understatement. There are numerous how-to books on the market with appealing titles on the order of *Internet for Dummies, Windows '95, Surfing the Net the Easy Way, How to Build the Perfect Computer,* and of course the all-time favorite, *Working on Your Computer in Your Spare Time.* Purchasing a how-to book will not make you an expert, but it will help you understand computerese, so choose carefully if you have extra money left over after you have paid your tuition and gone into debt on your new computer.

Also take into account that the faculty in your program, unless you are in a technology doctoral program, may not know any more than you do and are still busy just trying to retrieve their e-mail on a monthly basis. This is the world where capital letters make a major difference if you want to get on-line and "chat" with someone whether they are down the street or around the world. Don't fear, you need not become a computer wizard, but you will need to become quite intimate with your personal computer, its operating system, its RAM and ROM, its "friendly" user's guide (a typical oxymoron), and of course its unnerving capacity to continually beep, quack, blink, flash lights, and ring bells. The mouse, keyboard, hardware, and your software all have the ability to crash, usually for no apparent reason and always at the most critical moments. All the foregoing information might be of practical value if it hadn't all become obsolete 10 minutes after this was written. This computer revolution changes everything faster than the human brain can comprehend.

A major suggestion at this point is that you upgrade whatever you are using as a computer. Don't wait until you actually have to start writing your dissertation; upgrade about a year in advance so you can become familiar with the basic word processing functions, memory storage, editing features, cut, copy, insert, and paste amenities, tools and tool bars, thesaurus, find and backup default systems, or lack thereof. Trying to unravel the inner sanctums when you are approaching deadlines will only add to your stress level and raise your already skyrocketing blood pressure.

What to Do With Floppity Flops
(aka Black Beauties)

Black beauties are the flat, black, shiny objects purchased in computer stores by the tens, twenties, and hundreds, labeled "formatted" and costing obscene amounts of money. (Sometimes they are gray colored, in which case we would call them "the Old Gray Mares," but most of you are far too young to remember that silly little ditty, so we'll stick with the originals.) These formatted beauties, also known as disks, are ready to slip into the empty slot in front of your computer. No, no, they don't go in the bigger slot, the one that holds those round disks with the hole in the middle, the one that slides out easily with the touch of a button. That's clearly the best place for your coffee mug.

What we are talking about is the narrow, horizontal, disappearing black hole that eats floppies then refuses to spit them out until all the "formatted stuff" has been efficiently erased. Should you manage to retrain your computer anatomy to actually accept information on a regular basis, we suggest you copy everything in sight at least three times. One for a home copy, one for an office copy, and one for a safety deposit box, or at least to be stored at a friend's house. Sounds silly, we know, but you'd be surprised how paranoid one becomes when protecting such valuable work.

The strongest word of advice is to think ahead. When you actually start writing the dissertation, you don't want to have to rewrite what may have taken you hours of blood, sweat, and tears. So buy a bunch of black beauties, save your work frequently as you go along, then back it up, and make an alias file and duplicate the file at the end of every working session. Store these beauties in the safest places you know: in fireproof tornado- and hurricane-resistant boxes tucked into deep safety spots that have a moderate temperature zone environment. The only way to slay this fear of having all your precious words disappearing into the ether net of the microchip-munching monsters is to make sure you have tucked your floppies into a safe, secure place, far from the whims of forgetful minds and Mother Nature.

Dealing With Rebellious Floppies
(aka Mutiny of the Beauties)

We personally know of some fears that became realities: Tom had his car stolen right after carefully placing his entire box of backup files into a secret compartment in the trunk; Allison watched in terror as a firestorm demolished her entire house one week after she completed her final class, organized all her materials, and gathered the strength to finally sit down and write; Roberto received a phone call that his backups were tested by his best friend who was storing them for him, and she told him they were all blank—nothing copied successfully. Can you imagine having a lightning bolt destroy your hard drive in one crashing, sizzling burst from the heavens? All of these events actually occurred with people at the same graduate school. Multiply that by all the graduate schools in the country, and you can manufacture some serious fears.

If you really want to rest easily at night after spending 20 hours inserting those pesky tables from your statistical analysis, or after creating a particularly brilliant section of critique, make a printed hard copy of your work. It is often easier to review, and cut and paste, if you can spread the papers out on the desk or floor to get an overview of your organization. It will also be easier to recycle that piece of paper when you finish your work than to re-create something that was a "fluke" and a stroke of genius to begin with. This paper chasing method is guaranteed to prevent your temptation to ram your boot right through the windows when all information disappears into a black hole.

Statistical Analysis
(aka The Numbers Game)

If you have a few statistical tables to impress your committee, and maybe even potential readers (face it, this is the one section most readers will skip), we suggest one of two things: Buy a program that runs stats (that way you also get the user's guide) or hire someone to do it for you. Here is a quick checklist to help you decide.

	Yes	No	Don't Have a Clue
1. Data sheets and decimal places depressing you?	_____	_____	_____
2. Histograms and correlations pushed you to the corner?	_____	_____	_____
3. Nodding off in the middle of the null hypotheses?	_____	_____	_____
4. Multiple regressions sending you into mental reduction?	_____	_____	_____

If you checked more than one yes or don't have any idea, buy a program or hire someone. When we suggest that you "hire someone," we are advising you to hire professional statistical programmers, not personal psychiatrists, although you might keep the name of a neighborhood "shrink" on your desk. We believe that what you do on your own time is entirely up to you. Frankly, we just hope you have some private time to mess around and navigate in new templates and numlocks. It would certainly be relaxing and may even stimulate enough energy to allow you to return to work on the dissertation.

Qualitative Coding
(aka Put Out More Flags)

It would only make sense in this ever-changing world that someone would look for an easy way to analyze the mountains of notes and reams of transcribed interviews that you collect using a qualitative strategy. Gone perhaps are the days when it is politically correct to carry paper bags, boxes, binders, and journals with you as evidence that you are analyzing your data, although there is something quite physically invigorating in displaying to your beloved significant others, as well as other doctoral students, the great lengths you have gone to and the sheer volume of rich and deep data you have amassed. It just seems to make sense, now that there are computerized programs claiming they can and will "help you build a better relationship with your data," "support processes of indexing, searching, and theorizing," and "improve your closeness with your data."

Upon a closer analysis of this powerful new tool that leads you to a false sense of security of actually being able to analyze your data quickly, we found a number of self-evident truths emerging. One, there is now a new vocabulary for the computer-challenged, words such as *merge utility, character style, hot keys, call-outs, partial data links, concordance, system closure,* and others too numerous and mind-bending to mention. Two, if you actually remember to put all your written text into the program format, only then can you use these tools. Three, computerized programs have a tendency to quantify your qualitative data but, in some cases, as with methods in ethnography and possibly grounded theory, this may be a real advantage. And, four, you still have to know your qualifiers, have some idea of the overall themes to search for, and even need to know what your subthemes may be—not to mention your need to know the existential relatives to the subcategories. Ah, if only we could program the computers to actually think for us!

Most doctoral students we have spoken with have not mastered enough of the computer basics to achieve a comfort level with the pretasks, skills, or fundamental competencies with their friendly computer that are necessary for this level of data analysis. It takes you well beyond the use of the computer as a word processing tool. You now enter the land of utilities far beyond any expectations you may have. And always remember, if you are at home beginning to work with a new program, that friendly adviser isn't around to whisper in your ear, "No, dummy, you don't use that font key to cross your platforms." Neophyte computer users, and most of us are, may have a difficult time making these programs work unless they have practiced on predissertation writing. If you are comfortable with the type of analysis these programs offer, and believe your chosen program will meet your needs and your choice of methodology, then go for it.

Your biggest challenge might be to ask the computer program to determine what name your theme should have, but it might be easy, once you have identified your theme, to go through your text, via computer, to highlight or code those key words, thoughts, sentences, and paragraphs that apply to that theme. (Think what fun you have missed in struggling with those pages of written and typed notes and the floor space you will save by not having those unsightly piles of pages lying around.)

Do we recommend a computerized program for the analysis of qualitative data? It's hard to say. We believe that the beauty of qualitative data is in reading and rereading and physically manipulating the data, in discovering those little nuances, those pearls of wisdom your participants have orally bestowed upon you, and, of course, those missing four minutes of unrecoverable data that exist because your tape recorder broke down. There is something in the whole system of qualitative data that is rewarding when the system works exactly as it is supposed to, when people say exactly what you want to hear, in the exact words you want them to utter, but if you think everything will work this well, you are probably one who believes babies come from the cabbage patch.

Computerized data analysis programs can expedite your analysis process but they also create an atmosphere of "I'm even dumber than I originally thought!" If you can approach the use of these types of programs with confidence that you can master the computer's language, understand and use that language at more than a passable level, and like to spend more time in front of that fuzzy little screen, then certainly try out what is available. Just do it well before you face the deadlines for completing your data analysis, and remember that *practice* is a key word here. It will greatly ease your anxiety and help you maintain that tenuous level of sanity.

Getting a Life (aka The Good, the Bad, and the Ugly)

The "good" part is making time and space for your work. We suggest you begin each computer working session (remember, you have already scheduled an appointment with yourself for this time) with plenty of peripherals. These come in the form of potato chips, soft drinks, mints, or other appropriate refreshments; a straightback chair with a wide seat to support your overloaded brains in an upright position and to allow for the expansion of your seat area over the months you will be sitting; and plenty of room for those piles of papers you will make. You will need to explain to your devoted pet that you no longer can play at will, that cold noses on knees are no longer acceptable, and that no amount of sad, doggy-eyed looks will deter you from your goal.

You will want to set up your computer working area close to bathrooms and away from children's play areas and large-screen televisions, and be sure to leave room for high-intensity lamps to assist you in viewing your screen, especially if you have chosen one of those portable laptops with a small, 7-inch screen. An additional consideration may be the purchase of an intercom system that will respond to your cries for food and water, and be sure that the responder has the ability to put any meal into a one-handed sandwich form.

The "bad" part comes in when you worry about losing information. Get with the program you are using. Find out how to construct a table of contents the easy way. Make your spell checker your intimate friend. Allow for download time, especially if you didn't understand 2,400, 4,800, or 9,600 baud when you purchased your modem. Understand that memory is no longer a function of your top-loaded human appendage but a big bunch of bits and bytes that can turn you off when you try to save all that hard work you have just accomplished in constructing and analyzing your data.

Use multiple disks for different portions of your dissertation. In this way, if you happen to lose one disk, you at least don't have your entire dissertation at risk. You will have to do more cutting and pasting, but the loss of a disk or the all-too-familiar note on the screen that alerts you to "disk error" will not cause a complete mental meltdown. An easy way to arrange the disks is to have one disk for the actual chapters you are writing, one disk for the pre-pages and bibliography, one disk for data analysis, especially if you are conducting statistical tests of significance, and one disk for miscellaneous. It is important to remember that most computer word processing programs have a feature that will allow you to paginate between files, so you don't have to store the entire 300 to 400 pages in one file.

And the "ugly" part can be pretty personal. First, there's no reason to carry your dissertation disks with you at all times. It is certainly tempting, but carrying the load of papers you have to haul around is enough to convince naysayers that you actually are accomplishing something. You are already suffering from Dissertation Dementia, no need to add to the symptoms by becoming known as that crazy person who needs a disk-ectomy surgical procedure. Second, life in the computer room has been known to create sallow complexions, extreme fatigue, and dark circles under the eyes. You may even experience gastrointestinal distress, upper and lower back pain, and respiratory illness. These are not fatal and should be treatable after you remove yourself from the environment. Your appearance may become haggard, you may forget to shower and wash your hair, you may notice your clothing is mismatched or unkempt. Other common symptoms may include insomnia or hypersomnia; peculiar eating habits including binging, fasting, or forgetting to eat; lack of interest in pleasurable activities; and a total withdrawal from any social interaction that does not involve other doctoral students.

Diagnosis of this temporary disease involves many clear signs. You may express open aggression and hostility toward anyone (except a committee member, of course) who questions your dissertation topic or methodology. You might find yourself babbling when forced to converse about anything other than your topic. You may even find yourself sitting motionless in front of a computer screen rereading the same sentence for hours. Some have been known to sleep with a style manual under their pillows, hoping to absorb nighttime vibes of writing pearls. The most common sign, of course, is carrying a current draft of your dissertation with you at all times—to the grocery store, to the cleaners, out with friends for dinner.

Other signs include a phobia of losing things, especially articles for your literature review, and grandiose delusions that include the belief that the dissertation has some significance and will be the next number one best-seller. Do not despair, many documented cases of Dissertation Dementia have been known to disappear immediately after the defense date when the newly crowned doctor returns to a normal sanity level and joins the ranks of the unemployed.

Do not despair; physical activity is a terrific reliever of the stresses of academia. We suggest you do your level best to maintain a regular exercise program and healthy diet. For your emotional stability, and to reenergize your creative juices, we found some of the best methods are sneaking off to an occasional movie, browsing through bookstores (the fiction section, of course), searching out any light and lively entertainment, and staying in touch with friends in the real world.

We Can Survive This Challenge (aka Save Our Sanity)

It's an old story now, but we will repeat some obvious ways to save your sanity as well as your dissertation. You know to save everything as you write it, and to make copies on a regular basis, say every 10 pages or so. You compulsive, anal-retentive types will already be punching "save" every couple of sentences, anyway. Just hope you live long enough to see the finished product! We suggest you print out hard copies at every opportunity, and store them at several locations, because if the worst happens—lightning, stolen car, amnesia, or firestorm—at least you can scan them back into the computer.

Of course you techno-wizards know that a scanner is not to be confused with a "scammer": A scanner is a big, flat machine that allows you to feed your hard copies back into the computer and so save your behind and those few brain cells you have left if you burn up your hard drive; a scammer is someone you often meet while trying to get sane in the local watering hole for discouraged dissertation students. Your computer program with the "save and store" technique works only when you remember to use it. So, skip the paranoia, let go of the irrational obsessive-compulsive behavior, write a bunch of stuff, save it, print it out, hide it in a tree trunk, then run back in the house/office/lab and write a bunch more. Most things that you worry about are not going to happen, but if you must worry, worry about those big disasters and what you can do to prevent them.

What Not to Write
(aka Scarlet Letters)

Making notes is an art form happily acquired by the obsessive compulsive, the forgetful, the terminally bored, and the overworked doctoral student. It is a method of survival that is highly recommended by the three of us as well as most other crazies who have embarked on an adventure as long and arduous and frustrating and potentially rewarding as a doctoral program.

Notes serve only one basic purpose: They are terrific reminders for cloudy brains. And they have only one basic need: They must not be misplaced or lost. Unfortunately, this is precisely what most notes tend to do during their short lifetimes. They wander away on sturdy little legs to gather dust or to wreak havoc. If you are going to go to the trouble to make notes, at least have some form of storage system that makes retrieval a reality.

Future Vision

If you are like most of us, your notes are written as reminders of future responsibilities. This works beautifully if you remember where you put the note that tells you where you are supposed to be tomorrow at 9:30 and with whom you are meeting. You may prefer to stick it on your computer, mirror, day-timer, a nearby coworker, your own forehead, or any other readily accessible body part (preferably your own). You only have to be able to find it when necessary. Such compulsive note-taking also works well for assignments, times for research gathering, meetings, and anything else important enough to keep pounding into your brain. Most of us love these notes and have turned the writing of them into an art form.

On Liberty: The Present

Writing notes in the present tense may seem like a waste of time because you are very busy living moments, not stopping to record them. In research, however, and in the process of putting together the Big D, writing notes may well become second nature to you. Interview notes, field notes, observations, and impressions are all considered important. Notes about people you just met, conversations, places, directions, and ideas to think about—the possibilities are infinite.

A friend of ours has a "Snibbles File" just for ideas and thoughts that pop into her head as she is driving, walking, daydreaming, teaching a class, chasing tardy children through the neighborhood, or trying to balance her checkbook. She writes down far-fetched thoughts and ideas on small notepads that she tucks into her pockets and purse until they finally come to rest in a fat file at home. This Snibbles File has been the saving inspiration of many an unfinished paper and the beginning sentence of some of her most exciting stories. Whatever your use of today's notes, the written words represent ideas and concepts that may tickle your imagination into successful writings or doings. It's a habit worth cultivating.

Blackbeard's Ghost: The Past

This is where notes take on a power of their own. Some of those comments in your own version of a Snibbles File may be the ghosts that lead you into or out of trouble. It is well known that your e-mail, personal letters, phone calls, and meetings can all be reconstructed by the Techno-Wizards Who Search for Ghosts. These can be used against you, of course, if you tend to be a nasty-minded or incriminating note-taker who lets his or her notes wander off, but they also may be used to help you wiggle out of an argument, prove a point, solve a mystery, or keep you out of a misdemeanor charge.

And this is another nifty secret. When you are writing the dissertation, and turning it in to your committee members in pieces or chapters, make notes and keep copies of their comments and suggestions. It is apparently common for these Powerful People, who can control your future with the stroke of a pen, to (gasp!) actually change their minds about what they want you to write—one version this week, another next month, a third version months later, then, surprise, back to the beginning when she or he admits, "I guess it's better the way it was. Change it back."

Your notes, your copies of their ideas jotted in the margins, and your smart saving of all their past and present notes may enable you to survive the writing process and encourage your committee to honor your previously agreed-upon time line. And don't be afraid to use these reminders. We all get absentminded sometimes, and the busier we are, the more befuddled we tend to be. So use these blackmailing notes nicely, perhaps even gently, but do take a stand to remind your adviser(s) that you have changed that paragraph (or section, or chapter) so many times it no longer bears any relationship to the rest of the dissertation and may you please finish this endless rewriting before you enter Blackbeard's kingdom of ghosthood?

One last reminder about the latest form of note-taking—electronic mail. We are all aware that computers are invaluable for reaching into libraries around the world to access obscure, abstract, and ancient information that you may want to include in your dissertation. Computers are also invaluable for reaching out and touching someone at any time of day or night by electronic mail, and therein lies the rub (pun intended). There is a reason we subtitled this section "Scarlet Letters." E-mail is terrific, fast, concise, and worldwide. E-mail can also be dangerous, libelous, and downright dirty, and many people simply don't stop to think about this. The cybercops are seldom on duty, and emotions and hormones tend to rage uncontrolled when messages are written anonymously.

It is best to remember that e-mail is neither private nor secure. The information superhighway, in spite of the techno-wizard claims, has sections that are still like an old country road: narrow and winding with ruts, potholes, and detours. Take the hint and don't send any scarlet letters to friends, fellow students, or professors that you wouldn't mind being read by anonymous folks when the information superhighway delivers them to the wrong address. This is when the scarlet part becomes flamed, and that's the last thing you need to be dealing with when in the middle of a dissertation. Unless this is how you like to get your jollies, of course. In that case, flame away, it's absolutely no business of ours.

The stronger or the more suggestive the note, the more likely you are to remember it. And the more damage it can do later. Scarlet letters live many lifetimes.

It's About Time
(aka In the Home Stretch)

If a doctoral student makes the decision to hire a professional dissertation typist, she or he will need to get the working draft onto a computer program. There are many thesis and dissertation typists who will only accept computer disks as a condition of service. Be prepared to pay per page for this service and realize that additional costs are accrued for those elaborate tables and figures you have so thoughtfully designed to enhance your dissertation. Be sure to thoroughly interview the typist before hiring to find out if he or she is familiar with your particular institution's forms and formats. You may want to check with your graduate division for a list of those persons who frequently work with these types of documents. Many typists will not do editing but will provide such services as being sure your citations in the text match your references. Of course, many editors do this as well.

If you choose to do your own word processing and typing, you must figure in a generous time allowance to complete the task. An advantage or disadvantage of undertaking this immense challenge is that you can continue to edit your writing as you go along, but be sure that you have your style manual at hand and your university's guidelines nearby. There have been some dissertation defenses in which the main topic was the failure to follow form and format. Know the functions of your tool bars. They can and will save you many minutes, which add up, in performing necessary functions. Don't forget that on most word processing programs, the edit window allows you to change your mind or undo the function that you have just performed, but you have to do this as your immediate next step. Ask for advice freely from other doctoral students regarding your computer dilemmas, but be sure to start the conversation with the question, "Are you using MAC or IBM?" Finally, know the location of and directions to your nearest computer superstore, preferably open 24 hours a day, so that you can easily make those "at a moment's notice" trips. Purchase supplies in twos or threes so you can limit your 2:30 a.m. trips. The bottom line is this: If this chapter only confused and frustrated you, sometimes it is just better to hire the service and take that two-week break you desperately need and so richly deserve.

SECRETS CHECKLIST

1. _____ Save everything at least three times and keep it in three different places.

2. _____ Don't purchase a whole new computer system the day you want to begin writing your dissertation.

3. _____ Know the basic language of the computer you are using. Add the words *save* and *backup* to your everyday vocabulary.

4. _____ Make sure you have a "computer techno-wizard" for a friend whom you can call 24 hours a day.

5. _____ This is not the time for creativity in selecting far-out fonts, underlining, bold print, or off-beat sizes. Decide what you will use—usually dictated by your university—and stick with it. Academia does not consider Zauf Dingbats or Comix Heavy to be acceptable fonts regardless of their zippy looks.

6. _____ Know what is expected of you before you begin: manuscript margins, proper paper, specified font and size, exact format, lined-up quotes, and graphs.

7. _____ Scarlet Letters

   A. If it's incriminating, don't write it down, unless it will keep you out of jail.

   B. Have one place for all your notes—a place only you can access, like a Snibbles File.

   C. Keep copies of all correspondence from your committee—you're going to need them if you want to complete this project in one lifetime.

9

Defending the Dissertation

(aka The Power and the Glory)

The day will come when this chapter will become the reality of the steps you must now take. There are plans to be made and procedures to be followed to ensure that you actually are conferred upon (yes, that is what they call it) that diploma that bestows upon you those three little coveted letters (actually it is two big letters, a couple of periods, and a small letter, but it is still impressive). You will process additional paperwork, cajole committee members to clear busy calendars, apply for graduation, and, of course, make plans for life after the Big D.

It is important to remember two rules that all bureaucracies have: One, the paperwork never seems to be done, and, two, there will seem to be as many pieces of paper to process at this point as you have used in writing your dissertation and recycled. Check once more into those last few pages of your doctoral handbook. Review the deadlines for defense dates for each term; memorize the deadlines for announcement preparation; and, more important, begin to sweet talk the person who is responsible for preparing this announcement of your impending freedom. Find out the deadlines and costs for submitting final copies for binding, and oh, we almost forgot, find out how much it will cost you for printing and binding those multitudes of copies that you promised everyone when you finished. And you thought you were through with extra expenses!

Party Hearty (aka 'Twas the Night Before the Defense)

Some of the above rules and regulations will be in your doctoral handbook and some will be university-wide rules. It is wise to check with both your individual college, department, or school and your graduate division. Our institution had a whole set of papers just for the completing doctoral student. While you are at it, find out the protocol for the approval of your final chapters. Again, in our institution, all final chapters first went to the chair for final approval before they were given to the other committee members. There are advantages and disadvantages in this system.

The advantages are that if you have worked well with your chair and are confident the process will soon end, you will enjoy that last "stickie" note you can paste, with great satisfaction, on your chapters announcing "approved by the chair." Be absolutely sure that your style and format are up to speed. Questions at the defense are tough enough about your findings and conclusions. You don't want to spend any time during your defense discussing your lack of proper *APA*, *Chicago*, Campbell, or Turabian style.

The disadvantages are that the process is time-consuming. You will be responsible for the delivery of all documents, forms, papers, and miscellaneous items to various people (remember when you insisted on five committee members, naively believing it would better your odds?), and must remember where their offices are so you can hand-deliver these precious documents. If, on the other hand, you now face the task of just alerting your chair that you intend to finish in this life, you should go back and reread the chapters on selection of committee members and getting organized. Even at this point, our institution required that two weeks before our defense date, we submit two copies of our final dissertation to the faculty office so that other faculty members could have the opportunity to review the work. And, yes, as you suspected, they all now get the opportunity to "nudge" their opinions into the picture.

Don't be surprised by the final hoops you must now pass through, prior to being absolutely finished. (Type A's will be in organizational heaven and Type B's will be in a never-ending nightmare.) You may get such wonderful readings as Copyright Rules and Regulations (including an application form and a request for fees); University Microfilm Incorporated Procedures (including an application form and a demand for fees); and lists that need signatures verifying you have indeed presented bound copies to your university, graduate division, each committee member, and possibly your individual division (this usually doesn't have an application form attached, but it certainly implies fees to be paid). That is another point to consider, the cost of making copies of your 400-page dissertation. Find out who is responsible for making these copies and the cost for those additional 10 bound copies that you promised to all your friends and relatives as proof you are now learned.

We found that we could save money if we copied the pages ourselves, but the book binder then told us to be absolutely, positively sure that all the pages were in order and facing the right way. They took no responsibility for this small matter. Find out the type and weight of paper that must be used; some require all on watermark, 20-lb. paper, and some only require the original on this type and weight of paper. Find out—don't assume—whether your graduate division has joined this century and will accept colored copies of some of those wonderful graphics or pictures you have developed (be sure also to find out the cost of printing in the wonderful world of color).

Finally, find out who and with what half-ton truck these documents will be transported to the copy center, the bindery, and then back to the university community. We know of a doctoral candidate who left town shortly after completing his defense and final revisions. The bound copies of the dissertation were delivered to the university per prior arrangement and sat in a box on the floor of the mail room until after the deadline for submission had passed. It seems that no one had taken the responsibility (or was even remotely curious) to find out what was in the box, why it was there, and, in fact, no one even questioned the rather large, obtrusive object that sat on the floor for over a month blocking the path to the mailboxes. Remember, you were naive enough to actually think that all you had to do was write the thing. If you need any assistance with any of above, we suggest you refer back to the chapter with the section on Scarlet Letters.

The Final Hours
(aka The Sense of an Ending)

Now it's time to do your final preparation. Take your chair to dinner, offer wine and refreshments, and ask what will happen the next day. Does she or he foresee any problems, are there any last-minute concerns, and will the committee be there? If the answers are not what you expect them to be, you still have a few hours to prepare yourself. Select your clothing well in advance, be aware of the temperature in the room in which you will defend, and realize that you will most likely be standing half the time and sitting half the time. Now is not the time to break in those new shoes or try to squeeze into that great pair of pants or skirt that need a safety pin to hold up the waist line. Practice your presentation only once and then forget it. Take a long meandering walk, swim a few laps in the pool, or soak in a hot tub with a glass of wine. Just unwind and spend a quiet remainder of the evening with no stressful interruptions.

As you have already followed our previous advice and attended a few dissertation defenses, you know the general rules and lay of the land: The chair will open and establish the rules and guidelines for the session; you will talk about the work in which you are now the expert, using your 20 minutes of allotted time to convince everyone that your 400 pages of written text and 10 months of work clearly show remarkable originality and stunning conclusions. They may question your every move; you will confidently answer every parry and jab; they will finally say, "OK, no more questions, you can leave the room now," and they will proceed to talk about you behind your back while you wander about in a daze; you will then return for a final round, alone this time; and then you will exit as if the world has not just now changed.

A few sage words of wisdom for those final moments of subordinate servitude. As you begin to speak, first thank those in the room, particularly your committee (this will save you later, should the occasion warrant, writing those unmeaningful thank you notes); introduce any and all persons in the room to each other, if your chair has not done so; and take the opportunity to stand (this puts you in a proven dominant position, while all others are seated). And don't forget those who may have chosen to attend this session in support of you. Be considerate enough of their time to provide them with a copy of your abstract and maybe a copy of your research questions. Remember, they haven't seen the final results and will not necessarily know what the questions you are being asked are all about.

Your first words will be shaky but as you warm to your subject, you will remember all those important names of theorists; you will remember all that you have read, written, analyzed, and struggled with these many, many months. You will have practiced this defense in your mind at least a dozen times and are probably overprepared, but more is better than less.

The use of an overhead projector adds direction to your presentation and with the graphic programs now available you can come up with interesting bullets, borders, and creative ways to present your salient findings that up until now you were not allowed to use in your *APA* style. It will also give you a focus should you find your eyes straying out the window as you have a total block on your next words.

It is best only to present something similar to your abstract. Highlight your problem and purpose for the research. Reiterate your research questions and hypotheses, and identify the strategy or focus of your literature review, throwing in those now all-too-familiar names. You should briefly outline your methodological strategy of choice and then bring forth your most important findings, those that either have emerged or were found significant. End your discussion with your general conclusions or findings and your recommendations. You may now gracefully wilt into your seat.

There is no easy way to predict the first question, but once it is out of the way, approach all the questions as an expert witness in a panel discussion. This is your topic, your research; your opinions are just as valid as, if not more so than, anyone else's in the room. This really is a time for critical discourse about your topic and you should be well prepared to participate in the dialogue. Direct eye contact in answering each question is best; it also helps unstick you from your chair.

If someone throws a question you consider irrelevant to your study, you can agree, "Yes, that is an interesting question and would make a great topic for a follow-up study." Other times you will have to be more direct and say, "I chose not to follow that strategy or finding because . . ." (but move with caution here, you will have to use rational, academic reasoning in this type of response).

In any case, the questions will end and the audience may be asked to participate (ritual and tradition may vary here by institution). It doesn't hurt to have a member of your support group ask you that one vital question that you were so prepared for but no one bothered to ask. Don't be surprised if the questions asked by your committee don't seem even to remotely resemble anything you anticipated. Sometimes either the entire defense is taken up by discussion about a committee member's interest in your topic (especially if your topic is one that is highly politically correct) or they will describe various experiences of their own that they have somehow related to your topic. Your chair should be helpful here in focusing the attention back on you and the task at hand. If not, just ride it out, sit with that smile of confidence on your face, and interject if you get the opportunity.

Some candidates can get caught between disagreements among committee members that for some reason surface during the defense. It happens and there is nothing you can do about it. Posturing may be a hard habit to break for some. Look to your chair for support and, again, just sit it out. As with all good things, this, too, will end.

Expect and anticipate that you will have corrections, revisions, and rewriting to do. Imagine four or more people seeing something in its totality for the first time and not finding something wrong (in their opinion, and it still counts) or questioning one or all of your final conclusions. We are convinced this is part of the process; we all went through it and everyone who follows in the same footsteps will also go through it.

If, in those last few days before your defense, you find one of those "stand-out" errors like a word misspelled in your title or the name of one of your committee members misspelled, reprint that page and take copies to the defense. Give them to the committee prior to the defense call to order and briefly explain. They will assure you that they also caught that error but it will also let them know that you are on top of things and accountable. No dissertation is ever perfect, even after the bound copy is on the university library shelf. No spell-checker will catch every *if* that should have been an *in* or *is;* no grammar check will ensure that every sentence makes sense; and no editor can be 100% accurate. Accept this fact and it will make your life and life-to-be, postdissertation, more bearable. Forget the guilt; it is a complete waste of energy.

Celebration (aka The Agony and the Ecstacy)

It is important that among your lists of things to do near the end is to begin to think and dream about your celebration. You will want to end this journey with an exhilarating experience both directly after the defense as well as with loved ones and friends possibly at a later time. Don't assume that others will take care of this for you unless you specifically ask them. Don't let the opportunity get away to share in this exciting time. Find out the protocol at your institution for on-site receptions. It is thoughtful to have a champagne toast and light refreshments ranging from fruit to cookies to light snacks (cookies, brownies, and miniquiche are all good finger foods) catered in. Most university food services can and will help you with this for a very reasonable price.

Our alumni institution has now initiated the policy that they will provide the reception for a completing doctoral student. It's a nice touch. You can take it as is or supplement it by rewarding yourself. Invite all the professors you may have had to attend this reception; invite the office staff and particularly the secretaries to share in this with you. Bring a camera to record those "Kodak moments" and be sure to bring a small token of your thankfulness to those members of your support group, even if it is only a copy of your acknowledgment page where you have written those glowing words of appreciation for their unwavering support that has brought you to this day.

Be sure to get the extra copies of your announcements and, if you are particularly sentimental, ask for the pen used to sign your committee approval form. Find out if your chair will keep the signed copies or whether you should take them. Be gracious whenever anyone now addresses you as "Doctor" and say thank you. You can now afford the luxury of that small courtesy. Insist that your family and friends now call you "Doctor" for at least 24 hours. Propose a toast to your committee and to your long-neglected family and friends. Bask in your accomplishment and savor the moment. There are too few in life like these and you have now beaten the odds; you are no longer one of those more than 50% of ABDs. Tomorrow will be another day and you will now be postdoctoral (something like leftovers). Your 15 minutes of fame will slide over to the next doctoral student.

Whatever happens to you now, hold dear those wise and wonderful words of Sachel Paige, "Don't look back, something may be gaining on you."

SECRETS CHECKLIST

1. _____ Plan to complete all the paperwork and procedures the bureaucracy has listed for you to do.

2. _____ Take advantage of this ending to make it special, dignified, and glorious. Share this experience with friends, loved ones, and your committee.

3. _____ Help another doctoral student along the way with sage words of wisdom and advice.

4. _____ Strongly consider publishing what you have spent so much time on. Share with the world your findings and your revelations. It's a sad statistic that if you don't do something with your work within the first two years, you probably won't do anything with it at all.

5. _____ Celebrate!

10

Avoiding Sudden Stops

(aka Little Shop of Horrors)

In this final chapter we have gathered a few of the "horror" stories that have paralyzed students at various institutions. In addition to long-distance calls, we employed the time-honored method of data collection followed by Alice Roosevelt Longworth: "If you can't say anything good about somebody, sit right here by me." Sometimes discussing horror stories stops the repetition of the experience because those of you who may be closing in on final dissertation stages might get a bit twitchy about completing the work on time and tempers have been known to occasionally flare. We hope these vignettes will strengthen your resolve to prevent similar experiences.

Horror Story 1: What Proposal Defense?

Universities often encourage students to attend dissertation proposal and dissertation defenses. Announcements of these meetings are typically made in class. Three students decided early in their doctoral experience to attend one such dissertation proposal defense and were aghast when they were asked to leave the meeting. Apparently, the committee was shocked with the proposal and found the student ill-prepared for the defense. The committee did not want to embarrass the student by turning down the proposal so, instead, explained that the defense would be turned into a working session.

MORAL OF THE STORY

Apparently, some universities allow the student to publish the date of the supposed defense. As a well-informed student, plan ahead. Make sure that your committee chair states that you are ready for this important step. Don't embarrass them or yourself.

Horror Story 2: The Human Subjects That Went Awry

The Committee for the Protection of Human Subjects failed to approve a student's dissertation research proposal. The student made a couple of changes and went ahead with his interviewing, certain the committee would feel differently the next time they read the proposal. Unfortunately, the committee did not feel that the changes made were adequate and again denied the proposal. This student was lucky because he was not expelled from the program, but he had to start the dissertation over again.

MORAL OF THE STORY

Human Subjects Committees are very particular about the details of the dissertation. The rules and regulations must be followed so that no one is open to criticism (or lawsuits) later on. Read Chapter 4 again. You cannot and should not be sloppy on this issue. The rules are set in concrete. Just do it!

Horror Story 3: If at First You Don't Succeed

One student wrote three proposals, experienced three committees (one with each proposal), spent two extra years, and had major rewrites later. When she eventually finished, everyone was exhausted.

MORAL OF THE STORY

This woman has amazing determination. Not all of us are so lucky. But she had little planning ability and desperately needed this book. What happened to talking to other students and her committee members early on? Remember to discuss your topic thoroughly before you begin writing, again as you are writing, and again after you write the dissertation proposal.

Horror Story 4: Warning—Costly Detours Ahead

One student planned his defense date with his committee. Because he now lived a great distance from the university, he booked airline reservations, hotel room, and car rental a month before his date.

Two weeks prior to the dissertation defense, he was notified that his chair had not thoroughly read the dissertation and he was to forget the date. He also would need rewrites. The financial loss was over $500.

MORAL OF THE STORY

Inform your committee if there are significant costs involved in attending your dissertation defense. Make sure they understand that you cannot afford this loss. The emotional loss and the financial loss are two big issues that should not have to be dealt with. Take the time and effort to thoroughly discuss your expectations.

Horror Story 5: Yes, Virginia, Graduation Is an Important Date

One student had planned her intended graduation for two years. She felt her dissertation was in order because her chair had encouraged her to defend it. She was shocked to read a memo from a committee member to her chair two weeks before the date stating, "The fool has already ordered her cap and gown." And "the fool" graduated with honors, but the memory lingers.

MORAL OF THE STORY

Don't be discouraged by one committee member. Recognize that your chair has more power. When you are ready, let the others know you are ready.

Horror Story 6: Would the Real Chair Please Sign In

Six weeks before a student was to defend his dissertation, a committee member usurped the chairperson's role and announced to the student, "You can't graduate this spring. The graduation ceremony isn't important anyway, what do you care? You'll have to wait until August. Graduation ceremonies are overrated anyway." After this student recovered from the shock (only with a great deal of emotional support from his family and friends), he was able to convince his chair that he was indeed ready. He completed the work and his entire family flew in for the graduation ceremony (one from Japan).

MORAL OF THE STORY

This student insisted to his chair that he was indeed ready. Stand up for your work—fight for your work when you know you're ready. Be a politician when you get into trouble. And ask yourself, why didn't you know the secrets before you reached this point?

Horror Story 7: It Ain't Over 'til It's Over—Politics U

One student finished her course work, received the green light for writing the dissertation, and then the university yanked all financial support. They gave her teaching responsibilities to another student as well as her grants. This woman spent several weeks in Boston, in January, sleeping in her car or sneaking into a lab to sleep on the floor before she could get her financial picture back in focus.

> **MORAL OF STORY**
>
> Recognize that financial support can be changed according to the politics of the university. This student took two additional years of working and writing to finish. She acknowledges her family and friends for their support during this difficult time of her life, and we applaud her determination. Remember the chapter on student support? You may want to reread it!

Horror Story 8: They Shoot Horses, Don't They? Defenses From Hell

A young man completed his dissertation defense and was told to wait outside while the committee members discussed the necessary issues. Unfortunately, it was unusually cold outside where he was waiting and the one-hour delay was pushing the anxious student over the edge. It turned out that one committee member wanted the entire dissertation rewritten. The resulting discussion took the chairperson one hour until he prevailed over the upset committee member and all three signed the forms. Revisions were many, but the dissertation was accepted. He was able to complete the revisions after he thawed out.

> **MORAL OF THE STORY**
>
> Stay in touch with all committee members to help keep everyone actively involved in the process so that no one committee member keeps you guessing at the defense. It's all right to state ahead of time . that you are willing to do your part to prevent shocks in the defense, and if everyone has done their work, there won't be any. Each chapter should be read by all committee members in advance so that they can have any negative comments rectified before your big day!

Remember, even in the best of circumstances, you, the student, will never feel certain that your work will be accepted but at least if you have involved your committee members throughout the process by working out sticky areas of disagreement, a positive outcome is more likely.

Horror Story 9: Dueling Committee Members, Blazing Pistols

Two committee members got into a verbal, and almost physical, fight. The student felt they could not agree on anything and, to make matters worse, they forced the student to reschedule her defense to a later date.

MORAL OF THE STORY

Carefully check the reputations of your committee members. Academia is filled with politics. Know who gets along well and who does not. Talk to other students who have previously defended their dissertations using these professors. Be forceful with your committee members early in the process by explaining that you do not want unnecessary surprises at the defense. Try to get all of the problems resolved as you proceed so that you can rest assured that the process will move along as well as possible.

Horror Story 10: The Bionic Candidate— How to Finish Intact, on Time

One gutsy student interviewed his committee, assuring them it would be an honor, indeed a privilege, to serve as members of his dissertation committee. They accepted his chutzpah without comment, and the team worked well in their journey to a scholarly and well-written dissertation.

MORAL OF THE STORY

A few students do not need this book. This individual understood the dissertation process. He finished on time with a minimum of hassle. His experience truly was a happy ending to a process including good preparation. You, too, can have the same positive outcome if you are willing to apply these *secrets* to your dissertation process.

We wish you good luck and good writing now that you know the necessary secrets for a successful dissertation.

Emergency
Appendectomies

Appendix A

Action Words
to Introduce Quotes

— shows
— challenges us to consider
In their book, — explore
— goes beyond the idea that was preached in
True quality elicits, in —'s words, "love . . ."
—, speaking at a conference, said
In his essay, — challenges the conventional view
A recent article in — contrasts the approach to that of —
— calls the theory of — the most important contribution to —
— was the subject of research by —
He adds:
— underscores
—'s idea of — is underscored in his writing
— characterizes his views on
From —'s perspective
— suggests that
In his book, — details

As — chronicles in his book

In his book, — provides a sobering assessment of

— views the economic policy as

— in his book — documents

In —'s view

In forsaking history, many people in business are, to paraphrase
  philosopher George Santayana, "condemned to . . ."

— published her analysis of

A report by —, published in —, showed

A lesson from — is that

— has demonstrated that

— introduces the idea of

— wrote about

To paraphrase —

— calls this —

In —, Drucker provides an analogy

— writes

— suggests that

In an article —, Paul worries that

— asks

— is trying to create what he calls

— notes

In —, — describes

— explains

— uses the concepts of — to provide counsel

Consultants like — incorporate the ideas of — in their writing

— writes

He adds

— makes the point

— warns

—, who —, emphasized

— are using models of

—, in —, introduces notion of

— suggested that

—, which — calls —

— believes that
— researched
— has written extensively about
In the book, — reports on
— addressed the need for
— reported that
— has suggested
— is explored by —
— spoke to the world council, "Indigenous people are the base . . ."
— shows what — will do
— argues for
— argues against
— presents arguments against
— evolves the theory of —
The theory of — evolved from the work of —
An article in — discussed
— observed that
— points out that
— examines
It is apparent to — that
— has evolved the idea of
—, from his study on —, concludes
As shown by —,
In —, — looks at
For —, there seems to be
— is credited with
The importance of —'s thinking comes from providing a logical
  process
— bases her ideas of — on —
In providing a reasonable argument for —, —
— continues by saying
— vision is reflected in the words
— take a third position
— resolves the issue by showing —
— argues further that

According to —'s theory,
— clearly elucidated
— further sees
— defines
— summarized
— devoted space to
— gave a one-sentence definition
— articulated a distinction
— attempted to
— used the works of — to show
The same point is made by —'s conviction that is shown in
— reiterated
— clarifies
— uses the example of — to show
For —, leadership is —
— reflected on
—'s model allows
The dominant idea, theme understanding, in — is that
— has long held
—'s reaction to — is
— dismisses the idea of —
Using the framework of —, it can be seen
— concluded the talk by
— summarizes
— postulates
— queried
— predicted, warned, advised, anticipated
— words typify
—'s research heralds a new
—'s theory of — reveals
— conjectures, proposes, suggests
— speculates, surmises
— puts forth
— alludes to
— enlightens

—'s work informs us about —
— directs attention to
— broadens the understanding
— is convinced
— expounds
— interprets
— qualifies
— illustrates
— contributes to
— promotes the idea that
— affirms the view that
— reasons that
— substitutes — for —
— portrays, illustrates, delineates, depicts, charts
— deliberated on
— believes that
— cogitated on
— surmised that
— understands that
— realized that
— considered
— speculated on
— rationalized the — by
— pondered
— weighed
— applied
— examined
— perceived
— discerned
— distinguished
— recognized
—'s reply to, response to, rejoinder to
— regarded
— was concerned with
— recounted, related

— referred to
— drew a parallel to
— touched on
— was concerned with
— referred to
— repeated, reiterated, echoed, reworded
— conceived the idea/notion that
— mused about
— viewed
— comments, remarks, gives voice to, asserts
— exhorts us to
— accentuates
— is credited with
— gives credence to
— acknowledges that
— questions, inquires, explores, probed, analyzed, grappled with
— studied
— appreciated
— envisioned

Appendix B

A Research Proposal:
A Checklist of Items for Possible Inclusion

The following is a checklist for items that are typically included in a research dissertation or report. Not all of the suggested categories are necessary or appropriate for all studies, and the order of the items may vary somewhat. These items are only intended to serve as a guide.

Chapter One: The Problem

_____ Introduction

_____ Background of the problem (e.g., educational trends related to this problem, unresolved issues, social concerns)

_____ Statement of the problem situation (basic difficulty, area of concern, felt need)

_____ Purpose of the study (goal oriented)—emphasizing outcomes or products

_____ Questions to be answered or objectives to be investigated

_____ Conceptual or substantive assumptions (postulates)

_____ Rationale and theoretical framework (when appropriate)
_____ Delineation of the research problem (explication of relationships among variances or comparisons to be considered)
_____ Statement of the hypothesis (conceptual rendition subsequently followed by operational statements in Chapter One or in the "Methodology" chapter)
_____ Importance of the study—may overlap with statement of the problem situation
_____ Definition of terms (largely conceptual here; operational definitions may follow in the "Methodology" chapter)
_____ Scope and delimitations of the study (narrowing of the focus)
_____ Outline of the remainder of the thesis or proposal

Chapter Two: Review of Related Literature

_____ Organization of the present chapter—overview
_____ Historical background (if necessary)
_____ Purposes to Be Served by Review of Research Literature
_____ Acquaint reader with existing studies relative to what has been found, who has done what, when and where latest research studies were completed, and what approaches involving research methodology, instrumentation, and statistical analyses were followed (literature review of methodology sometimes saved for the "Methodology" chapter)
_____ Establish possible need for study and likelihood for obtaining meaningful, relevant, and significant results
_____ Furnish, from delineation of various theoretical positions, a conceptual framework affording bases for generation of hypotheses and statement of their rationale (when appropriate)

NOTE: In some highly theoretical studies, the "Review of Literature" chapter may need to precede "The Problem" chapter so that the theoretical framework is established for a succinct statement of the research problem and hypotheses. In such a case, an advance organizer in the form of a brief general statement of the purpose of the entire investigation should come right at the beginning of the "Review of Literature" chapter.

Sources for Literature Review

_____ General integrative reviews cited that relate to the problem situation or research problem such as those found in *Review of Educational Research, Encyclopedia of Educational Research,* or *Psychological Bulletin*

_____ Specific books, monographs, bulletins, reports, and research articles—preferences shown in most instances for literature of the past 10 years

_____ Unpublished materials (e.g., dissertations, theses, papers presented at recent professional meetings not yet in published form but possibly available through ERIC)

_____ Selection and arrangement of literature review often in terms of questions to be considered, hypotheses set forth, or objectives or specific purposes delineated in "The Problem" chapter

_____ Summary of literature reviewed (very brief)

Chapter Three: Methodology or Procedure

_____ Overview (optional)

_____ Description of research methodology or approach (e.g., experimental, quasi-experimental, correlational, causal-comparative, or survey)

_____ Research design (spell out independent, dependent, and classificatory variables and sometimes formulate an operational statement of the research hypotheses in null form so as to set the stage for an appropriate research design permitting statistical inferences)

_____ Pilot studies (as they apply to the research design, development of instruments, data collection techniques, and characteristics of the sample)

_____ Instrumentation (tests, measures, observations, scales, questionnaires)

_____ Field, classroom, or laboratory procedures (e.g., instructions to subjects or distribution of materials)

_____ Data collection and recording

_____ Data processing and analysis (statistical analysis)

_____ Methodological assumptions

_____ Limitations (weaknesses)

_____ Possible restatement of conceptual hypotheses from "The Problem" chapter in operational form relative to instrumentation and experimental procedures or design followed (operationally stated hypotheses can also be put in null form to furnish an optional third set of hypotheses amenable to statistical testing)—if not done elsewhere

_____ Summary

NOTE: The *proposal* may have a "Time Line for Completion of Project" section.

Chapter Four: Findings (Analysis and Evaluation)

_____ Findings are presented in tables or charts where appropriate

_____ Findings reported with respect to furnishing evidence for each question asked or each hypothesis posed in problem statement

_____ Appropriate headings are established to correspond to each main question or hypothesis considered

_____ Factual information kept separate from interpretation, inference, and evaluation (one section for findings and one section for interpretation or discussion)

NOTE: In certain historical, case study, and anthropological investigations, factual and interpretative material may need to be interwoven to sustain the interest level, although the text should clearly reveal what is fact and what is interpretation.

_____ Separate section often titled "Discussion," "Interpretation," or "Evaluation" to tie together findings in relation to theory, review of literature, or rationale

_____ Summary

Chapter Five: Summary, Conclusions, Recommendations

_____ Brief summary of everything covered in first three chapters and in findings portion of Chapter Four

_____ Conclusions ("so what" for findings, often the hypotheses restated as inferences with some degree of definitive commitment and generalizability)

_____ Recommendations (practical suggestions for implementation of findings or for additional research)

Criteria for Evaluation of a Research Report, Article, or Thesis

I. Title of article or report
  A. Precise identification of problem area, often including specification of independent and dependent variables and identification of target population
  B. Sufficient clarity and conciseness for indexing of title
  C. Effective arrangement of words in title

II. The problem
  A. Description and statement of problem
    1. Statement of basic (felt) difficulty or problem situation—significance and importance of the problem areas in either basic or applied research
    2. Careful analysis of known and suspected facts and explanation of existing information and knowledge that may have some bearing on problem—spelling out specific factors giving rise to the basic difficulty, spelling out their interrelationships, and their relevance to the problem area
    3. Soundness of the logic underlying selection of variables or factors to be studied and expression of their relationship to the problem area

4. Systematic and orderly presentation of the interrelationships of relevant facts and concepts underlying the problem
5. Clear identification of the problem statement through use of an appropriate heading or paragraph caption (the same requirement holding for other major categories of the research)
6. Succinct, precise, and unambiguous statement of the research problem (including the delineation of independent, dependent, and classificatory variables) of the major questions to be resolved or of the objectives to be investigated
7. Distinction (if required) between problems or questions that are either factually oriented or value oriented
8. Distinction in the instance of theoretically oriented research or of basic research between the purpose, which is often goal oriented or instrumental in relation to certain pragmatic objectives, and the research problem, which is primarily directed toward the finding of relationships, the making of comparisons, or the noting of changes (possible cause-and-effect relationships) relative to operationally formulated research hypotheses

B. Sufficient delimitation of the problem area—narrowing of the scope without becoming concerned with a trivial problem
C. Review and evaluation of the literature pertinent to problem areas
1. Adequacy and relevance of the previous investigation cited with reference to the basic difficulty posed, design of the current investigation, procedures followed, and projected analysis of data
2. Appropriate development of a rationale or framework from the research studies cited with reference to the current problem under investigation
D. Clear-cut statement of the conceptions, assumptions, or postulates underlying the problem being investigated
E. Precise statement of (a) hypotheses or (b) deduced consequences of theories or (c) the objectives of a study (objectives being most common in survey and descriptive research)
1. Hypotheses involving relationships and comparisons
2. Presentation of deducible consequences or predictions (if any) that are logically consistent with a hypothesis (i.e., antecedent-consequent statement: If A exists, then B follows)

F. Definitions of terms
1. Clarity in the definitions of key terms and variables (especially constructs)
2. Use of operational definitions whenever possible

III. Design and methodology (procedures)
A. Logic, structure, and strategy of study carefully delineated
1. Distinction made between whether the research involves variables manipulated and controlled by the investigator (usually found in experimental research) or whether an ex post facto situation exists involving the analysis of data already available or collected as in most field studies and correlational investigations
2. Appropriate use of paradigms, flowcharts, or schematic models
3. Specification of threats to external and internal validity of the design employed
B. Clear descriptions of samples studied
1. Mode of selection of subject cited (e.g., random assignment, matching voluntary participation, or convenience by being available)
2. Data regarding how representative a sample is relative to a population
3. Information concerning the possible operation of selective dropout and survival of the fittest
C. Adequate information pertaining to the reliability, validity, and standardization properties of instrumentation—psychometric characteristic of scales or tests used
D. Sufficient description of operational or field procedures followed in the collection of data—where, when, and how data were obtained
E. Coordination of the specification of the relationship between the null (statistical) hypotheses and the research (problem) hypotheses
F. Appropriateness of the statistical treatment and data processing procedures
G. Evidence of a preparatory pilot study having been conducted
H. Procedure clearly enough described so that other investigators can replicate (repeat) the study performed under essentially comparable conditions in the future

I. Statement of methodological assumption such as adequacy of reliability and validity of measures, representativeness of samples, fulfillment of appropriate requirements for carrying out statistical tests

IV. Presentation and analysis of data
   A. Logical and orderly exposition in terms of the framework of the hypotheses, deduction, objectives, or questions asked in conjunction with the statement of the problem
      1. Objective rather than subjective or speculative presentation
      2. Analysis consistent with and supported by the facts obtained
      3. Absence of overgeneralizations or sweeping statements that go beyond the data
      4. Relationships of the findings to previously cited research explicitly stated
      5. Negative findings relative to the hypotheses as well as positive findings presented with minimal distortion or bias
      6. Uncontrolled factors influencing data outcomes appropriately cited and discussed
      7. Weaknesses in the data honestly conceded and discussed with appropriate emphasis
      8. Lack of confusion between facts and inferences—clearly shown separation of analysis of findings from interpretation and discussion of findings
      9. Resolution of contradictions, inconsistencies, or misleading elements in the findings
   B. Appropriate and clear use of charts, tables, figures, and graphs

V. Summary and conclusion
   A. Precise and accurate statement of (a) the problem, (b) the methodology followed, and (c) the findings without the introduction of new or irrelevant information
   B. Conclusions at a scope and level of generality justified by the data presented
   C. Appropriate caution exercised and necessary qualifications made in drawing conclusions
   D. Conclusions in a form that other investigators can understand and subsequently verify

E. Conclusions coordinated with the tentative acceptance or rejection of the research hypotheses presented or with the objectives or questions posed

F. New questions set forth for possible investigation—recommendation for additional research in the problem area

G. Recommendations concerning implementation of the research findings when appropriate relative to the objectives stated in the purpose of the investigation (most frequently encountered in survey studies and action research)

SOURCE: Isaac, S., & Michael, W. B. (1995). *Handbook in Research and Evaluation* (3rd ed.). EdITS/Educational and Industrial Testing, San Diego, CA. Reproduced by permission.

Appendix C

Statistical Decision Tree

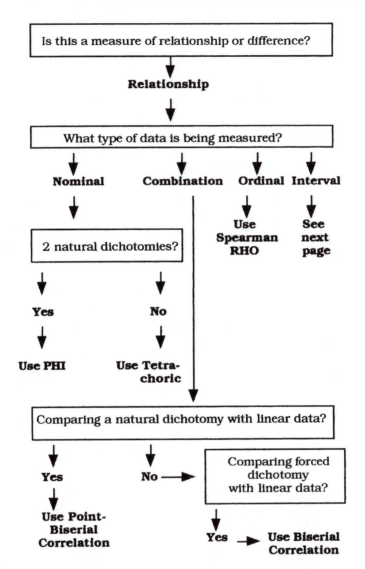

Figure C.1. Decision Tree: Choice of Appropriate Statistical Procedure
SOURCE: Adapted from Ron Jacobs, Ph.D., Professor, Rehabilitation Counseling, San Diego
State University; used by permission.

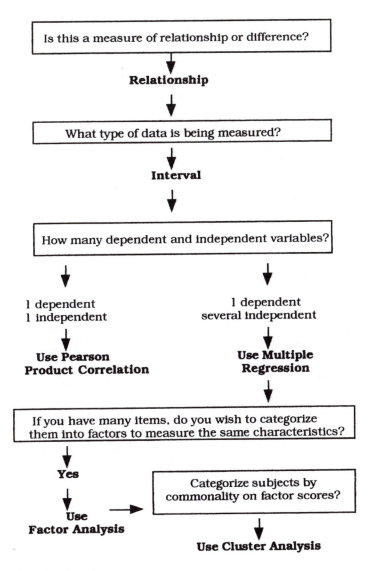

Figure C.1. Continued

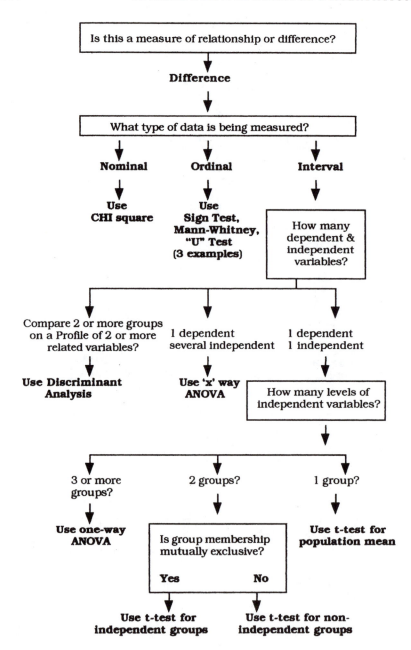

Figure C.1. Continued

Appendix D

List of Active Verbs

accentuates
acknowledges
addresses
adds
advises
affirms
allows
alludes
analyzes
anticipates
applies
appreciates
argues against
argues for
articulates
ascertains
asks
asserts
attempts

bases
believes
broadens
challenges
characterizes
charts
checks
chronicles
clarifies
cogitates
comments
compiles
conceives
concerns
concludes
condemns
conducts
conjectures
considers

continues
contrasts
contributes
convinces
counsels
creates
credits
deals
decides
defines
deliberates
delineates
delivers
demonstrates
depicts
describes
designs
details
devotes

directs
discerns
discusses
dismisses
displays
distinguishes
documents
draws a parallel
echoes
elicits
elucidates
emphasizes
encourages
enlightens
envisions
evaluates
evolves
examines
exhorts
expands
explains
explores
expounds
extracts
files
finds
follows
formulates
gathers
generates
gives
gives credence
gives voice
grapples
heralds

holds
identifies
illustrates
implements
incorporates
influences
informs
inquires
inspects
inspires
integrates
interprets
introduces
investigates
judges
leads
lectures
looks
maintains
manages
manipulates
mediates
models
muses
notes
observes
offers
operates
organizes
paints
paraphrases
perceives
performs
pilots
ponders

portrays
postulates
preaches
predicts
prescribes
presents
probes
promotes
proposes
protects
proves
provides
publicizes
publishes
puts forth
qualifies
queries
questions
raises
rationalizes
reacts
realizes
reasons
recognizes
recommends
records
recounts
recruits
reduces
refers
reflects
regards
reiterates
rejoins
relates

remarks	sees	talks
remembers	shapes	touches
repeats	shows	underscores
reports	speaks	understands
researches	speculates	unifies
resolves	states	upgrades
responds	stipulates	verbalizes
retrieves	studies	views
reveals	substitutes	warns
reviews	suggests	weighs
rewords	summarizes	worries
says	surmises	writes

Suggested Readings

Chapter 1: Writing the Doctoral Proposal

Locke, L. F., Spirduso, W. W., & Silverman, S. J. (1993). *Proposals that work.* Newbury Park, CA: Sage.

Offers specific and detailed advice for the proposal stage using strong examples for students to understand what works.

Chapter 2: Choosing a Methodology

Denzin, N. K., & Lincoln, Y. S. (Eds.). (1994). *Handbook of qualitative research.* Thousand Oaks, CA: Sage.

This book is a compilation of ideas, concepts, and theoretical bases for most of the qualitative methods. It is extremely useful in defending your choice of method as it gives you current theories and the operational workings of a chosen methodology.

Huck, S. W., Cormier, W. H., & Bounds, W. G., Jr. (1974). *Reading statistics and research*. New York: HarperCollins.

Yes, this is a statistics book! But it is fairly easy to read and gives the reader a comprehensive set of instructions on how to write (publish) results of quantitative research. It even gives you something similar to sentence starters. This book is also a good reference for the advantages and disadvantages of each statistical treatment, something you will need in defending your choice of methodology.

Leedy, P. D. (1995). *Practical research: Planning and design* (5th ed.). New York: Macmillan.

An excellent review for any kind of quantitative research. Its practical, no-nonsense approach makes the basics understandable to even the novice reader. It offers many charts that outline purpose, goals, and appropriate applications that make it difficult not to be successful in planning a good research study.

Lincoln, Y. S., & Guba, E. G. (1985). *Naturalistic inquiry*. Beverly Hills, CA: Sage.

All books by Guba and Lincoln are well worth reading. Their approach to evaluation will be useful for almost any research with human subjects.

Merriman, S. B. (1988). *Case study research in education*. San Francisco: Jossey Bass.

If you are conducting a case study, this book is worth purchasing. Merriman is often cited in qualitative dissertations and is regarded as a leader in the case study research field.

Miles, M. B., & Huberman, A. M. (1994). *Qualitative data analysis* (2nd ed.). Thousand Oaks, CA: Sage.

This book allows the qualitative researcher to view various methods of presenting data, mostly in a graphic format. It is unique in that it presents visual applications of data displays and helps the qualitative person stay within the bounds of qualitative reporting.

Morse, J. M. (Ed.). (1994). *Critical issues in qualitative research methods.* Thousand Oaks, CA: Sage.

A good overview of qualitative research methods with references at the end of each chapter so that further information on one specific type of research can be better understood.

Yin, R. K. (1984). *Case study research: Design and methods.* Beverly Hills, CA: Sage.

Another one of the "must-have" books for case study research. Yin is certainly recognized as an authority in the field, and the book itself is set up to be easily referenced.

Chapter 3: Selecting Committee Members

Myers, I. B., & Myers, P. B. (1980). *Gifts differing.* Palo Alto, CA: Consulting Psychologists Press.

This book will help you identify your personality type. You must know yourself before you can understand others!

Chapter 4: Surviving the Human Subjects Committee

Check your own institution's handbook for requirements.

Chapter 5: Collecting Data

Fink, A., & Kosecoff, J. (1985). *How to conduct surveys: A step-by-step guide.* Newbury Park, CA: Sage.

This one is an absolute must for those designing surveys or questionnaires. It takes an easy-to-understand approach, step-by-step, through the development of an instrument. It also gives the reader a great appreciation for the positives and negatives of survey research.

Glass, L. (1992). *He says, she says: Closing the communication gap between the sexes.* New York: Putnam.

You are most likely going to be interviewing both women and men, so you might as well have some basic information about gender communication styles as a starting point. Because the genders tend to be socialized differently, and have different coding and decoding styles, this information will help you structure both your questions and your analysis with more understanding and sensitivity.

Hawley, P. (1933). *Being bright is not enough: The unwritten rules of doctoral study.* Springfield, IL: Charles C Thomas.

Dr. Hawley's book is written from a student advocacy perspective. Her approach is personal and practical as she deals with the issue of ABDs. It is fairly easy reading but Dr. Hawley goes back and forth between her academic professorial role and that of a student struggling through the dissertation phase.

Reardon, K. K. (1995). *They don't get it, do they? Communication in the workplace—closing the gap between men and women.* Boston: Little, Brown.

Another excellent reference from the experienced voice of a specialist in negotiation and interpersonal communication. Reardon offers terrific communication ideas for research in business and leadership dissertations as well as in general communication patterns.

Chapter 6: Developing a Support Group

Gray, J. (1990). *Men, women, and relationships: Making peace with the opposite sex.* Hillsboro, OR: Beyond Words.

Communication is the foundation of all human interaction. Given that we deal with both genders in life, as well as in academia, we might as well understand the basic differences in communication styles.

Kroeger, O., & Thueson, J. M. (1988). *Type talk.* New York: Dell.

Type Talk discusses our basic personality types and offers suggestions for improving working relationships in mutually supportive ways. We learn techniques to resolve our differences rather than denying or ignoring them. Good for building committee relationships.

Sternberg, D. (1981). *How to complete and survive a doctoral dissertation.* New York: St. Martin's.

> This volume can be found only in your university library, which shows that some things never change. One of the best chapters is the last: "Beyond the Dissertation: Surviving It and Professionally Exploiting It." This offers encouragement and a bit of entertainment.

Tannen, D. (1990). *You just don't understand: Men and women in conversation.* New York: William Morrow.

> This is a popular book, found in all bookstores in paperback. If you only wish to read scholarly books, this may not be for you—but it offers valuable communication tips for both genders.

Chapter 7: Getting Organized

Gordon, K. E. (1983). *The well-tempered sentence.* New York: Ticknor and Fields.

> For the "innocent, the eager, and the doomed," all of which fit doctoral students at varying stages of the writing process, this book offers punctuation guidelines with humor, stories, and clever illustrations that make the information both readable and rememberable.

MYSTAT Statistical Applications, Course Technology, Inc., One Main Street, Cambridge, MA 02142.

> This computer program is available in both MACINTOSH and IBM/PC versions. The user's guide is excellent in explaining data entry and also in giving examples of data problems. The graphics in the program are a bit more friendly than in STATVIEW (to be discussed later) but data entry is not as user friendly. Most statistical treatments are available.

O'Conner, P. T. (1996). *Woe is I.* New York: Putnam.

> The book cover proclaims it is a "grammarphobe's guide to better English in plain English," which it is, but it is also a clever, complete, delightful little volume with examples that make learning basic writing rules more fun than you thought possible.

Rudestam, K. E., & Newton, R. R. (1992). *Surviving your dissertation.* Newbury Park, CA: Sage.

This sage book contains a great deal of valuable information from the faculty viewpoint. You will find that the *Secrets* book is written from the student viewpoint and will make you smile and lighten your load. Together, you can't lose.

STATVIEW SE + Graphics, Abacus Concepts, Inc., 1984 Bonita Avenue, Berkeley, CA 94704.

A computer program designed for the Macintosh user that contains a comprehensive and easy-to-comprehend user's guide. This statistical program is easy to use and has a variety of graphics. Data entry is easy to understand. Most statistical treatments are available.

Strunk, W., Jr., & White, E. B. (1979). *The elements of style.* New York: Macmillan.

This book has been around for a long time because it is so useful. Reminders to cut unnecessary words, to use active verbs, and answers to all questions about punctuation are only a few of the book's offerings. This book should sit on everyone's desk and be used often, no matter how well you write.

Style Guides

The Chicago manual of style (14th ed.). (1993). Chicago: University of Chicago Press.

Publication manual of the American Psychological Association (4th ed.). (1994). Washington, DC: American Psychological Association.

A must if your dissertation must adhere to the APA format.

Turabian, K. L. (1987). *A manual for writers of term papers, theses, and dissertations* (5th ed.). Chicago: University of Chicago Press.

Condensed (and easier to follow) version of *The Chicago Manual of Style.*

Any other style manual accepted by your individual institution—and don't forget any style publications that may be available from the graduate division and/or those published by your individual college, department, or university.

Chapter 8: Using Technology

Any manual for your word processing system.

Your local phone book with dog-eared pages for computer stores, emergency services, and 24-hour techno-wizard referral hot line.

Chapter 9: Defending the Dissertation

Elgin, S. H. (1987). *The last word on the gentle art of verbal self-defense.* New York: Prentice Hall.

An excellent resource for building confidence, freeing yourself from verbal abuse, and learning how to avoid negativity as you elicit desired responses.

Walker, B. A., & Mehr, M. (1992). *The courage to achieve.* New York: Simon & Schuster.

This is the only study conducted on academically gifted women. It teaches women to honor their intellectual gifts and use them with no parental or spousal preapproval or approval.

Index

About the Authors

JACQUELINE FITZPATRICK, Ed.D. Jacqueline is Adjunct Faculty for graduate students in the School of Education at the University of San Diego. She supervises and mentors student teachers in elementary schools throughout the San Diego area. Jacqueline earned her doctorate in Educational Leadership with her dissertation research on the mentoring of professional women. Her presentation at the 1996 World's Future Society concerned women's contributions to leadership. Jacqueline previously taught in elementary schools, has been an educational counselor to high school students, taught research techniques in the Master's Counseling Program, and is currently working on her next research project addressing the concerns and experiences of women in undergraduate education.

JAN SECRIST, Ed.D.   Jan wears three professional hats: She is Adjunct Faculty at the University of San Diego (Master's Counseling, Extension and University of the Third Age), specializing in Life Span Development, Gender Communication, and Women's Issues; she has a private practice advising high school students in the college selection process; and is a seminar trainer for the U.S. Navy on Communication and Gender Issues. Jan gave a presentation at the World's Future Society on "Leadership, Gender and the Future" and frequently consults with business organizations on communication concerns. Jan's dissertation research has inspired two manuscripts: the narratives of midlife women, and a children's book. She plans further research on women's development.

DEBRA J. WRIGHT, Ed.D.   Debra is Associate Director and Program Administrator for the International Educational Leadership Graduate Program and is Assistant Professor teaching research methods and process at San Diego State University in California. She earned her doctoral degree in Educational Leadership from the University of San Diego, California. Debra has previously worked as a principal in an alternative high school and taught for 14 years in public education. Her research interests include issues of diversity and the process and methodology of research for educators. She has published articles related to nontraditional graduate education programs and student advocacy issues and produced instructional videotapes on the development of research proposals and theses.